Airbus A340

Philip Birtles

PLYMOUTH PRESS

Ian Allan
PUBLISHING

CONTENTS

First published 2000

ISBN 0 7110 2685 8 (Ian Allan Publishing)
ISBN 1-882663-43-8 (Plymouth Press)

© Philip Birtles 2000

Published by Ian Allan Publishing

an imprint of Ian Allan Publishing Ltd, Terminal House, Station Approach, Shepperton, Surrey TW17 8AS.

Distributed in the United States of America by Plymouth Press Ltd,
101 Panton Road, Vergennes, VT 05491.
Call: (800) 477-2398 or (802) 877-2150

Printed by Ian Allan Printing Ltd,
Riverdene Business Park, Molesey Road, Hersham, Surrey KT12 4RG.

Code: 0001/C

Front cover: In October 1992 China Eastern ordered five A340-300s, with the first A340-313 delivered on 15 May 1996. B-2382 is seen on the flight line at ready for delivery on 25 July. *Airbus Industrie*

Back cover: On 10 November 1998 Air Tahiti Nui took delivery of A340-211 F-OITN which had previously served with Air France as F-GLZD. *Airbus Industrie*

Above: The A340-500 evolved from a need from the airlines for an ultra-long-range airliner with the capacity of the A340-300. The A340-500 therefore retains the same fuselage as the -300, but married to the new wing and Trent 500 engines for the -600. *Rolls-Royce*

Title page: Swissair is becoming an all-Airbus fleet operator and has ordered five A340-600s with options on four more. *Airbus Industrie*

INTRODUCTION

The Airbus A340 is the first airliner produced by Airbus Industrie with four engines and also optimised for longer ranges. It is however very much a part of the family of airliners making the best use of current and future technology, the computer hardware fitted being easily adaptable with advances in software to meet the market needs of the future.

Although launched as a joint project with the twin-engined but otherwise similar high-density medium-range A330, the A340 is now gaining its own reputation and market identity as a cost-effective ultra-long-range airliner capable of unrestricted operations over the longest routes. This is particularly on transpacific services from Asia/Australasia to the American West Coast, where even the best Erops (Extended-range operation) twin-engined airliner may be restricted due to the non-availability of suitable diversionary airfields. Many of the Boeing 747-100/200s were ordered for their long range, but did not need the high capacity on many of the long thin routes, making the A340 an ideal and highly cost-effective replacement for these early 747s. The planned Airbus A3XX even higher capacity jet airliner is projected at a totally new high-density long-range market.

With its future developments, the A340 will have the capability of flying around the world with one stop. The passengers will therefore have to endure long periods in the air, requiring greater levels of comfort. Airbus Industrie is offering lower-deck sleeping areas, lower-deck toilets, and increased pitch between the seat rows in all

Above: The Airbus A340-300 test-bed is the first long-range four-engine airliner to be produced by Airbus Industrie and the European partners. *BAe Airbus*

Above: In September 1992, Philippine Airlines (PAL) ordered six A340-200s with options on another four. However, operational and economic problems resulted in these aircraft being delivered initially to Cathay, and eventually passing to PAL when Cathay took delivery of its own aircraft. PAL also ordered four A340-311s, but with serious financial problems the airline has had to become practically a domestic operator. A340-313 F-OHPJ, leased to PAL from Airbus, was delivered on 30 May 1997. *Airbus Industrie*

classes, including economy. It is quite clear that the airlines earn their main revenue from the premium and business class passengers, and it may be that the full-fare-paying economy class passengers may have an improvement in comfort, but those people who seek even lower bargain fares may find themselves in a more dense fourth class. These decisions are all finally made by the airlines, who have to decide their profit margins.

In compiling this book I have had the willing help of many people, including the marketing organisations of many of the airlines who operate the A340, and my old friends at Airbus Industrie: Barbara Kracht; General Manager, Press & Information Services; and David Velupillai, Regional Manager, Press Relations; both of whom I know from my days in PR at Hawker Siddeley at Hatfield. Kristin Ronningsen in the Airbus Press & Information Services was very helpful with her supply of photos. Ann Bennett of British Aerospace Airbus at Filton kindly arranged for my transportation to Toulouse, which was probably made easier as I am still on the BAe payroll — as an early pensioner. While at Airbus, Barbara and David introduced me to Adelhard Leege, who enthusiastically briefed me on the latest cabin features and configurations; Alan Pardoe, Product Manager A330/A340, who outlined the marketing strategy for the A340; and Geoff Thomas, VP

General Engineering, who outlined the challenges of producing the A330/A340, as well as the new challenges of the ultra-long-range A340-500/600. Geoff started in the Tech School at Hatfield shortly after I did.

Apart from my own collection of pictures, and those supplied by Airbus and the airlines, thanks also go to David Charlton of BAe Media Services at Filton for the A340 wing production photos, which are particularly important due to the sophisticated engineering involved. Finally, as far as photos are concerned, I would like to thank my good friend, Nick Granger, who always manages to add his own fine selection of pictures to make the product that much better.

Finally, although the production list came from many sources, I would particularly like to thank John Roach for his help in completing the many gaps and ensuring the greatest authenticity. As always, my wife, Martha, has been very supportive, and on her travels around Asia has been known to capture some excellent pictures. I also appreciate the enthusiasm and support of the editorial team at Ian Allan, who always manage to turn my pile of material into a very presentable publication.

Philip Birtles
Stevenage, Hertfordshire
July 1999

1. AIRBUS INDUSTRIE

In the mid to late 1950s the British aircraft manufacturers were still not much reduced in capacity from World War 2, and were chasing ever-decreasing orders from a modest civil and military home market. Following the Comet 4 programme, de Havilland realised that for its next airliner project to succeed, there would have to be some risk sharing. As a result, the World War 1 company of Airco was re-formed, with de Havilland as the major partner, and joined by Hunting Aircraft at Luton and Fairey Aviation at Hayes. The programme was the DH.121, later to become the Trident.

In 1960 most of the British aircraft companies were merged into three groups, to achieve what de Havilland had intended with the Trident, and the company became part of Hawker Siddeley Aviation. This was itself some 20% of the Hawker Siddeley Group, a large industrial organisation. Hunting became part of the British Aircraft Corporation (BAC), and Fairey joined Westland Helicopters. Only Short Bros, Scottish Aviation and Handley Page remained independent, and Handley Page soon closed down.

However, the consolidation of the British aircraft industry was not enough, as, although rationalisation resulted in many site closures over the years, there was still a fundamental need to create a larger 'home' market to compete in particular with the strong American manufacturers, who benefited from a number of major domestic and international airlines capable of placing significant launch orders for new aircraft.

The Hatfield design team therefore started looking for European partners, initially in France, where there was also a strong established aircraft industry. BAC and Sud Aviation showed how to collaborate internationally with the Concorde programme. Although it was not a commercial success, it was certainly a great technological achievement, and because of the joint organisation it was impossible for one government to cancel, without the agreement of the other. However, there were no proposals for joint working on the much more commercial Airbus programme.

In July 1965, following informal discussions at the Paris Air Show, the major parts of the German aerospace industry formed Studiengruppe Airbus, the first time the name was used. Sud Aviation, Breguet and Nord Aviation had already been studying larger new jet airliners and later in the year the French government provided support for them to continue studies, although there was no clear specification from the airlines.

By 1965, the British and French manufacturers had begun to collaborate, but Sud was too busy working with BAC on the Concorde programme, and was not enthusiastic about starting another joint venture. However, Henri Ziegler of Breguet was very keen and as a result the HBN Group was formed by Hawker Siddeley Aviation, Breguet and Nord, with the British team being based at Hatfield where wing design was centred.

The Hatfield team began looking at new aerofoils with the lift more evenly spread across the wing surface, reducing drag and improving efficiency for a thicker and less swept-back structure. This supercritical aerofoil, as it became known, was lighter and provided more room for fuel, giving additional range. There were some delays when Breguet became part of Dassault and Nord merged with Sud to form Aérospatiale, the latter being decreed by the French government to be the national airbus partner.

In early 1966 the first meeting was held between the British, French and German governments to approve the national industrial partners of Hawker Siddeley, Sud-Aviation — soon to become Aérospatiale — and Arge Airbus. The favoured design was the big twin fan-engined HBN.100, which was to evolve into the Airbus airliner. Following the first joint board meeting of the partners, financial support was requested from the three governments for a 300-seat aircraft known as the A300.

The French government pushed for design leadership, which was agreed by the British government, provided the proposed Rolls-Royce RB.207 was the chosen powerplant. Following the first ministerial meeting, a joint project definition study was agreed, with the airframe research and development being shared between Hawker Siddeley Aviation (37.5%), Aérospatiale (37.5%) and Arge Airbus (25%). Meanwhile, Rolls-Royce would take a 75% share of the engine, with

12.5% taken each by Snecma of France and MAN of Germany. The initial market was estimated to be some 250 aircraft, with orders expected from the national airlines of BEA, Air France and Lufthansa. The formal Memorandum of Understanding (MOU) was signed between the governments in September 1967, with design expected to be complete by mid-1968, allowing a go-ahead for production. A major and significant condition for approval of the project was that the three national airlines would place launch orders for a combined total of 75 aircraft.

The overall aircraft continued to grow in size, the fuselage diameter being 19ft 7in (5.97m) and the length growing to 176ft 11in (53.92m) by mid-1968. Meanwhile, competition was coming from the USA and Britain, the American requirements resulting in the trijet TriStar and DC-10, while BAC proposed the Two-Eleven and later the Three-Eleven, with a pair of rear-mounted Rolls-Royce RB.211 engines, also offered for the TriStar. Due

to doubts about the RB.207 engine, and the bankruptcy of Rolls-Royce, the Airbus partners decided to scale down the proposed airliner so that it would be powered by two of the currently available Pratt & Whitney JT9D or GE CF-6-50 engines. The fuselage diameter was established as 18ft 6in (5.64m) and the overall length reduced to 158ft 6in (48.3m), the aircraft being called the A300B. It was to have the engines in pods slung under the low-mounted swept wings, with a conventional tail and fuselage-mounted tailplane.

In May 1969, the French and German governments approved the go-ahead for the building of the first aircraft with systems and engine commonality with the American DC-10, but meanwhile the British government in March elected to pull out of the programme, the reason being the lack of specified launch orders, leaving Hawker Siddeley on its own with the design of an advanced wing. As a result, Hawker Siddeley decided to invest its own resources in the design,

Above: Although Airbus Industrie started out as a one-product organisation with the A300B, it has now increased to seven distinct airliners with a number of variations. The original A300B, F-OCAZ, featured a global map on the forward fuselage showing the regions covered during development and the sales tours. Originally registered F-WUAB, this aircraft first flew on 28 October 1972 and is seen at Dublin in July 1974 as it arrives for a demonstration to Aer Lingus. Soon afterwards the aircraft was withdrawn from use and broken up at Toulouse. *Author*

Above: Air France was the first airline to take delivery of an Airbus with the first full-production A300B2, F-BVGA, on 10 May 1974. It entered service to London Heathrow from Paris on 20 May 1974, and has recently been dismantled at Hurn following retirement. *Author*

Above: The second of five A300B2s, D-AIAB, was delivered to Lufthansa on 19 March 1976, and visited London Heathrow on 23 March, prior to services commencing from Frankfurt on 1 April. *Author*

Above: An early and important American customer for the Airbus was Miami-based Eastern Airlines. The second aircraft for the airline, A300B4 N202EA, was delivered on 19 November 1977 and is seen on approach to Orlando, Florida, in August 1988. *Author*

development and production of the main wing-box, in effect becoming a subcontractor, leaving all the commercial decisions to the French and German partners, and resulting in many British companies not being selected for the supply of equipment and systems.

Airbus Industrie was finally set up with a Paris headquarters in December 1970, with the French and German shares at 46.7%, and the remaining 6.6% held by the Dutch government. Spain later took a 4.2% share, reducing the French and German holding. The main operating base of Airbus Industrie, including training and customer support, was set up at Toulouse, to be close to the Aérospatiale final assembly and equipping of the Airbus family.

The maiden flight of the first A300B was from Toulouse on 28 October 1972, the airliner achieving certification in March 1974, allowing service entry with Air France on the Paris-London route on 23 May. For some time Air France was the only customer, with a fleet of six A300B2s, even though there was no direct competition from America. The nationalisation of the British aircraft industry into British Aerospace on 1 January 1978 allowed an agreement to be signed at industrial level for the Airbus partners to consist of Aérospatiale, Deutsche Airbus, CASA and BAe, and government approval was achieved in October, giving Britain a full partnership in the programme. The shareholdings were then adjusted to 37.9% for Aérospatiale, 37.9% for MBB, 4.2% for CASA and 20% for BAe, confirming the wise business decision made in 1969 by the Hawker Siddeley Board to stay in the programme.

Above: The first A340-300 is compared at Toulouse with the narrow-body A320, and the wide-body A300-600 and A310, all assembled in the Aérospatiale facility for Airbus Industrie. *Airbus Industrie*

9

2. TECHNICAL DESCRIPTION

Above: British Aerospace Airbus at Filton, Bristol, and Hawarden, Chester, has design and production responsibility for the wings for all the Airbus family. The design was initiated at Hatfield until transfer to Filton in 1992 and the main assembly jigs have always been located at Hawarden. The wing skins are numerically control (NC)-machined on vast fixed flat beds with the cutters running on tracks either side. This top skin for an A330/A340 is held down by vacuum. *BAe Airbus*

Above: A substantial underfloor cargo hold is accessible from a large upward-opening door in the starboard front fuselage just aft of the forward retracting twin wheel nosewheel undercarriage. This example is on Singapore Airlines' (SIA) A340-300E, 9V-SJO, on pre-delivery preparation at Toulouse in June 1999. *Author*

Having established the initial Airbus specification, the next aim was to produce a family of airliners to compete in the world markets dominated by the giant American manufacturers. Over the next 30 years, Airbus Industrie grew from a one-product company with no market share, to a family of seven airliners with a total of nearly 1,700 orders, delivering on average one airliner every day, bringing major competition for Boeing. The wide-bodied fuselage width had been established from the start with the original A300 allowing use of standard LD3 cargo containers side by side in the underfloor hold, followed by the two-crew cockpit A310, and fly-by-wire (FBW) controls with the narrow-bodied A320.

In April 1985, the priority was to decide whether to produce an aircraft with two or four engines. As a result of a six-month survey with the airlines, the fuselage lengths were becoming closer together, providing a basis for a common design with a similar wing with the inboard engines at common locations. The A340-300 and A330 have identical fuselage structures. The A340 was Europe's first four-engine wide-bodied long-range airliner, the sixth airliner type from Airbus, although in numerical sequence it was the seventh. The reason for this is that both the

Airbus A330 and A340 were uniquely developed together with similar structures and systems, and although the four-engine A340 was the first of the new-generation Airbuses to fly, it was felt more logical to number the twin- before the four-engine aircraft. By developing the two aircraft together, the combined development costs were some $3 billion, instead of $5 billion if developed separately. The biggest challenge was to produce a single structure to meet the market needs for capacity and range, with available engines. The requirement was to meet the objectives of maximum take-off weight and balancing the common wing with the fuselage cross-section and length. This new airliner was aimed at part of the Boeing 747 market covering ultra-long ranges on thin routes which would not be economical for the Jumbo jet. Some 60% of the early 747-100/200s were bought for their range capability rather than their size, resulting in them often flying part empty on the long thin routes. The A340 is therefore better optimised for carrying 300 passengers over long ranges. It probably took the stretch of the original 5.64m diameter fuselage almost to the limit. The joint programme was launched by Airbus in 1987 with the same workshare as on previous types, despite strong opposition even from within parts of the organisation, but with launch orders from UTA as the lead customer, plus Air France, Lufthansa, Sabena, Air Inter and Northwest. In the event, UTA was merged with Air France and did not take delivery of its aircraft, which went to Sabena and later Air France, and Air Inter was also later absorbed into Air France. Northwest later cancelled its order for A340s as deregulation resulted in smaller aircraft being flown at greater frequencies.

The initial production version of the A340 was the -300 with a range of 12,500km (6,750nm), carrying 295 passengers in three classes. The shorter A340-200 is capable of carrying 262 passengers over 14,000km (7,560nm). The A340-200 was designed first as the ideal aircraft for city pairs, and stretched to the -300. Airbus believes that for ranges of over 10,000km (5400nm) the four-engine configuration is more efficient because the wing-bending relief provided by the two outer engines gives a weight saving of around 8 tonnes over a twin. A substantial underfloor cargo volume is available,

and can accommodate the universally available LD3 container.

With the first A340 in final assembly in mid-1991, certification was set for December 1992 and first deliveries to Lufthansa in January 1993. The total sales were 94 firm orders with the largest from Northwest placed for 20 aircraft in 1987. In addition to Lufthansa, Air France, Sabena, Iberia and Air Portugal had ordered the A340 for the longer-range routes where it is more economical than the Boeing 747.

Design studies began in the mid-1980s for projects known as TA9 and TA11 to satisfy the two roles, and by 1988 the aircraft were so similar in size that common airframes were a logical answer. It was essential that the wing would be efficient in both medium- and long-range operations, and the improved bending relief of the pair of outer engines allowed the wing to support more fuselage weight without increasing the stressing of the wing-to-fuselage joint. This would mean that a further 41,700 litres of fuel could be carried in the wing centre-section, providing the required additional range.

Above: A cargo door is also fitted for access to the rear underfloor cargo hold, seen on Air Canada A340-300 C-GDVZ/F-WWJV 'No 278' at Toulouse in June 1999 and delivered on 28 June. *Author*

Above: To cope with the greater all-up weights, the long-range A340 featured a centreline two-wheel undercarriage unit, as fitted to A340-300E 9V-SJO of Singapore Airlines. *Author*

The new types made increased use of composites and introduced aluminium-lithium in non-fatigue-sensitive structures, major advances in manufacturing technology, an advanced central maintenance system, and significant improvements in the fly-by-wire control system developed for the A320.

The A340-300 fuselage was the longest built by Airbus at the time, which at 63.7m was 10m longer than the A300-600. The stretch was achieved with three forward and four aft section plugs either side of the centre-section. The A340-200 is 4.3m or eight frames shorter. The identical geometry of the original A300B2 was retained with the location of the fuselage frames, floor beams and stringers unchanged, although advantage was taken of advances in materials and jointing to improve corrosion protection. The fuselage consists of a conventional aluminium monocoque structure with sheet metal frames in areas of normal loads, and machined frames in higher-stressed areas such as the wing-to-fuselage centre-section. The sheet-metal-formed stringers are open-section, hot bonded above the window line and riveted below. The majority of the fuselage skins are formed from sheet metal apart from the high-stress areas around the lower centre-section, where they are machined. The rear fuselage pressure bulkhead has been made more accessible for inspection against corrosion.

To retain as much commonality as possible with both types, each aircraft features a box-section keel beam, which is faired over on the A330 but supports the centre undercarriage unit of the A340, with doors and local reinforcement. It was more costly to add on items but it does allow optimisation of both aircraft in the integrated programmes. The A340 centre-section fuel tank is available for later range increases in the A330, and also common to both aircraft is the tailplane trim tank and computerised fuel system developed on the A310. This adjusts the centre of gravity position automatically to minimise drag, saving about 1.5% in cruise fuel burn.

The A330/A340 are totally Computer Aided Design (CAD) paperless aircraft, providing the data for Computer Aided Manufacture (CAM). The

A330 is a progressive development of the earlier A300, while the A340 is a natural extension to the family with the four engines best suited to long-haul, but it can equally be used economically for short to medium routes if required.

The large aerodynamic fairing under the fuselage/wing centre-section introduced a new hybrid carbonfibre/glassfibre-reinforced plastic structure to optimise weight while retaining enough impact resistance from stones thrown up by the undercarriage. The introduction of aluminium-lithium saved some 14% over conventional alloys, but lack of knowledge about its fatigue performance inhibited its use in high-stress areas. The initial area of its use was in the wing fixed leading edge 'D' spar, but fatigue testing was expected to allow further use of the material later in production.

The CASA-designed and built tailplane is produced entirely from carbonfibre-reinforced plastic (CFRP), and because of the large size of the A340, the individual port and starboard units are joined in the centre by a light alloy box instead of being bonded together as on the smaller A320. Tailplane drag is reduced by the introduction of a thinner aerofoil section and a new cambered profile, reducing the relative size. Apart from some local reinforcement, the fin is the same as the A300-600 and A310, saving money by allowing the use of existing jigs and giving design commonality across the wide-bodied types.

The common wing for the Airbus A330/A340 is the largest to be designed and built by British Aerospace, and has the highest sweepback at 30°, allowing higher cruise from Mach 0.82 to 0.84, compared with the earlier cruise of M0.80. Wing span over the winglets at 60.2m is similar to the Boeing 747-200, but the higher aspect ratio chosen to reduce both take-off and cruise drag gives a wing area of 362sq m, some 65% of the 747-200.

To achieve the multi-role wing there needed to be a close balance between the comparative bending moments exerted on the fuselage, to allow assembly in the same jigs. Design strength required for the A340 was only 1% more than the A330. Using the A300 wing experience, the structure consists of a load-carrying wing torsion box comprising front and rear spars linked by transverse ribs which support the top and bottom machined skins. An inboard centre spar, terminating outboard of the inner engine pylon, helps provide support for the large structure and allows for the more demanding damage tolerance. Although built in the same assembly jigs, the A340 wing has additional structural provision for the outer engines, which is left out of the A330 wing, resulting in them not being interchangeable.

Each wing has seven leading edge slats over the full span with gaps between the first and second, and fourth and fifth, to accommodate the engine pylons. There are two section ailerons which are drooped for take-off and landing to provide full-span trailing edge-flaps. The ailerons are deflected upwards on landing to increase lift dump and braking efficiency. The ailerons also deflect upwards when the inboard airbrake panels are deployed during manoeuvres to relieve wing-bending moments.

The overall aerodynamics of the wing are developed from the A310, featuring the same three-dimensional design, but adjusted for the longer ranges. Aspect ratio was increased from 8.8 to 9.3, and winglets added angled at 45° save an estimated 1.5% of fuel. It had been hoped to have identical pylons on inboard and outboard positions, but this proved aerodynamically unacceptable, although the inboard pylons were in the same location as on the A330. As a safety measure, the fuel collector cells, which provide the final fuel reserves, are located clear of any potential debris areas from an uncontained engine explosion. Another safety feature is that in the event of a survivable forced landing with the undercarriage up, the engines are designed to remain attached to protect the wing structure and avoid rupture of the integral fuel tanks.

The most important feature of any airliner is the cabin, because that is where the fare-paying passengers gain their impression of the aircraft. According to the airline requirements, the cabin can seat up to 295 passengers in a long-range three-class configuration, consisting of 18 first class, 81 business class and 196 economy class seats. At the other extreme is a high density A340-300 with 440 seats in a nine-abreast layout. The ultra-long-range A340-200 with the

Above: Computer-Aided Design (CAD) is used exclusively on the A340, providing the data for Computer-Aided Manufacture (CAM). The Airbus partners make a significant use of integral machining, rather than fabrication, which provides a greater accuracy and reduces assembly times. *BAe Airbus*

shorter fuselage can carry up to 262 passengers with 18 first, 74 business and 170 economy seats. For greater flexibility, an A340-300C Combi can carry up to 221 passengers with 12 first, 51 business and 158 economy, plus four main-deck cargo pallets. For the longer-range flights, an optional crew rest compartment is located at the front end of the rear cargo hold, based on a 2.4m pallet, and has been ordered by all operators so far. It is reached by descending a short flight of stairs, and there is an additional rest area just behind the cockpit. Passenger sleeper and lower-deck toilets are also an option available, but have not yet been adopted.

Entertainment systems are now a major customer feature on modern airliners, but have experienced difficult development, often because they are buyer-furnished equipment (BFE) and

therefore not properly integrated within the overall cabin systems due to a lack of clear responsibility. Airbus now takes full responsibility for the entertainment systems, although the airlines still have the BFE option. The new airline alliances will probably create a greater overall standardisation.

The cabin design is jointly developed by Airbus Industrie and the airlines using colours and logos to define the corporate identity. Airbus has been using a fully flexible cabin layout for some 30 years using the 1in pitch seat rails as the foundation for the galleys and toilets, referred to as monuments. In the areas of the monuments, seat rails have been subject to corrosion caused by spilt liquids and are difficult to replace. Airbus has broadened the flexibility of the cabin, and made the replacement of corroded sections

Above: Computer-Aided Design (CAD) is used exclusively on the A340, providing the data for Computer-Aided Manufacture (CAM). The Airbus partners make a significant use of integral machining, rather than fabrication, which provides a greater accuracy and reduces assembly times. *BAe Airbus*

Above: Once completed, the wings are mounted in pairs on a special jig for transportation to Hamburg to have the moveable leading and trailing edge devices fitted, before delivery to the final assembly facility at Toulouse. *BAe Airbus*

easier, by making wide structural provision and installing sections of seat rail in the areas where the monuments could be located. This also helps to reduce structural weight and with the introduction of vacuum toilets avoids the previously complex plumbing arrangement.

In the three-class configuration, the business class can vary considerably depending upon the route and destinations, while each class remains autonomous with its dedicated galleys and toilets. With the installation of the seat rail sections over broader areas, cabin adaptations can be achieved overnight for all operations, from scheduled to charter. During cabin design with the customer airline starting in the pre-contract stage, up to 90 layouts can be studied. The airline specifies the layout, including seat pitch, number of toilets and number of seats across the cabin. The cost per seat is the critical measure, consisting of the first cost, amortisation and

Above: The wings, like all other major sections of the Airbus family, are transported around Europe in a specially adapted A300-600ST Beluga. A set of A340 wings are being loaded at Hawarden with the forward unpressurised cabin section raised for access. *BAe Airbus*

operating costs, allowing the airline to charge a sufficiently low price to attract the passengers, while still making a profit.

All the current airlines have specified underfloor crew rest areas located in the forward end of the aft underfloor cargo hold. They provide six to seven bunks and the unit is based on the standard 96in pallet with full air-conditioning and electrics. These rest areas can be removed in 20min and installed in 40min if the aircraft is diverted on to a short- to medium-range route and needs more cargo capacity. In addition, the cabin crew who remain on duty have comfort seats installed in the galleys with retractable arms and partial recline.

For passenger use, to give stand-up headroom, the floor can be lowered in the keel area for a sleeping compartment with up to 10 beds on the lower deck in the rear section of the forward cargo hold. This feature can be installed or removed during a major check. It has not yet been adopted by any airlines as most airline first class seats now lie fully flat, and business class seats have full recline. In tourist class an option

is available for a fixed toilet installation in the rear underfloor cargo hold adjacent to the crew rest area. Within the module with toilets down either side of a vestibule, mirrors and washbasins are located at one end and there is better headroom in the toilets as the fuselage curvature is under the units. This makes long flights more acceptable to the passengers and frees up space on the main deck for additional seats.

The A330/A340 fly-by-wire (FBW) system is developed directly from the full-authority digital flight controls of the A320, but with significant changes as a direct result of that system's high reliability. The A340 has three primary and two secondary computers driving the flight control surfaces. Using three primary flight computers provides more redundancy and flexibility, and as the secondary computers have not had high usage in practice, they are a simpler type. In the unlikely case of complete digital flight control failure, reversionary control is provided to the rudder and stabiliser, with both digital electrical and direct mechanical linkage to the actuators. The A340 flight control system drives two

Above: The large under-fuselage/wing centre-section fairing is produced from a hybrid carbonfibre/glassfibre reinforced structure optimised for low weight and retaining impact resistance from any stones thrown up by the undercarriage. This is fitted to SIA A340-300E 9V-SJO nearly ready for delivery from Toulouse in June 1999. *Author*

ailerons and six spoilers per wing, together with the rudder, two elevators and trimmable tailplane.

The FBW system gives commonality across the Airbus family, allowing flexibility and savings on training costs. It normally takes five weeks to convert an experienced pilot to a conventional airliner, but after 13 days' conversion from the narrow-body twin-engine A320 on to the wide-body four-engine A340, it requires only one to three days to convert to the A330. Pilots enjoy the flexibility which gives better promotion and easier career opportunities. With the A330s

Above: The tailplane, designed and built by CASA of Spain, is produced entirely from carbonfibre-reinforced plastic (CFRP) joined together by a centre-section light alloy box. This tailplane is fitted to Air Canada A340-300 C-GDVZ/F-WWJV, MSN (manufacturer's serial number) 0278, delivered from Toulouse on 28 June 1999. *Author*

optimised for high-density regional routes, and the A340s for long-haul, the same crews can be used, ensuring they do not run out of currency on landings on the long-range flights. The FBW reduces hardware, manages change driven by the software and allows product improvement in service.

The digital flight-control system has two functions: the computation of the control laws, and sending the signals for control surface deflection. The two crew fly the aircraft through a side-stick controller, giving an uninterrupted view of the flight displays, the side-stick providing the overall command objectives in all three axes. The computers drive the control surfaces in response to the pilot's commands, but there is protection against excessive loading and significant departures from the normal flight envelope.

The A340 central maintenance system (CMS) monitors all aircraft systems, providing information to the flight crew, and when accessed by maintenance crew yields rapid means of displaying, interrogating and testing the systems for any faults. The CMS consists of two dedicated central maintenance computers, one being a live spare, with three flightdeck multi-purpose control and display units (MCDUs), and built-in test equipment (BITE) in each system. A flightdeck printer is available for maintenance use.

Left: Structurally the wings of the A330 and A340 are identical, but the A340 wing has additional provision for the attachment of the outboard engines, although the inboard engine locations are identical. The two CFM56-5C4 engines are seen under the port wing of SIA A340-300E 9V-SJO at Toulouse in June 1999. *Author*

Above: Centrally-located overhead stowage bins are supplied as an option in business class, and are normally fitted in economy class. The bins are articulated for loading and unloading and when stowed provide more headroom. *Airbus Industrie*

When a Class 1 failure is identified, the minimum equipment list (MEL) must be referred to and the failure is automatically displayed in real-time. Class 2 failures do not require reference to the MEL and no correction is necessary until the next visit to the engineering base. A Class 3 failure needs no attention until the next maintenance opportunity.

Airbus Industrie has been using the 'customer as partner' concept for many years in defining and producing its family of airliners. The only mock-ups are the cockpit to determine preferred layouts and the cabins to satisfy customer requirements. A systems test rig covers the operation and integration of all the systems, including undercarriage operation, ensuring software compatibility. A full-scale fatigue structural test airframe is located with Deutsche Airbus at Munich, with the static test specimen at Toulouse.

With the construction of a new assembly hall at Toulouse for the A330/A340, more flexibility and shorter build times are achieved. Work on the Clement Ader building started six months after the launch of the programme in 1987, with inauguration in October 1990, and the first A340 front fuselage was delivered a month later. The production layout is modular, with aircraft assembled independently instead of being dependent upon the build status of adjacent aircraft. The production rate was planned to build up to seven A330/A340 per month in 1995, and if demand is sufficient this could rise to 14 a month within the same facilities. The programme allowed 49 A330/A340s to be delivered in 1994, 81 in 1995 and 77 in both 1996 and 1997.

Final assembly uses approximately 4% of the total man-hours used to build the aircraft. Major innovations are the introduction of robotics for drilling the 3,500 holes for the wing-to-fuselage

Above: The rear galley of the A340 is well laid out and features semi-reclining cabin crew seats with arm rests to allow more rest during quiet duty periods.
Airbus Industrie

bolted joints, and automated riveting for joining the forward and rear fuselage sections to the cabin centre-section. The wing-to-fuselage mating activity takes about 35hr over three days. The resulting structure is lifted to the second main station, where the front and rear fuselage sections are attached in a cycle lasting around 12hr. At this location the composite tail and undercarriage are attached before the aircraft is towed on its own undercarriage to one of four cells for finishing and system testing, all the main system components having been installed before arrival at the Toulouse final assembly hall. After nine days in the cell, the aircraft is moved outside

for fuel flows and then into the customisation building for furnishing and fitting of the engines, followed by painting and preparation for flight.

The original work-share agreement was for the interiors to be fitted at Hamburg, but this meant fitting the engines and therefore paying for them, and then they remained idle for four weeks during customisation. To save this premature cost of the engines, all A320s, A330s and A340s are assembled and customised at Toulouse, and all A321s and A319s are assembled and completed at Hamburg, with DA retaining responsibility for preparation and packaging of the interior kits for Toulouse.

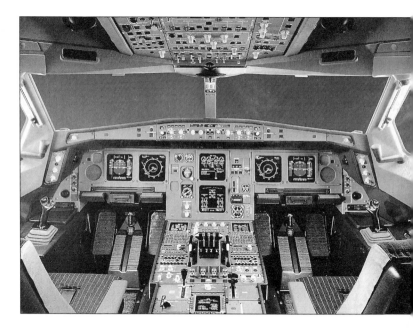

Above: The modern flightdeck of the A340 is practically identical with the twin-engine wide-body A330 and the narrow-body A320, apart from the four thrust levers and associated engine indicators on the central engine/warning display. The technology was developed on the A320 programme and features the side-stick controller — unique to these airliners — instead of the traditional control yoke. This provides an uninterrupted view of the instrumentation and a pull-out table is located below each of the Primary Flight Displays (PFDs) and Navigation Displays (NDs) which can be used by the crew for in-flight meals and charts. *Airbus Industrie*

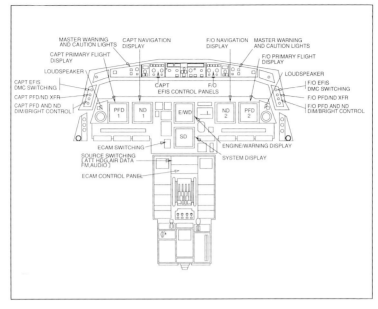

Above: **A340 cockpit arrangement.** *Airbus Industrie*

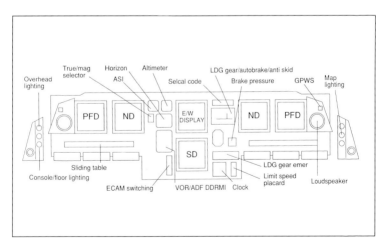

Above: **A340 main instrument panel.** *Airbus Industrie*

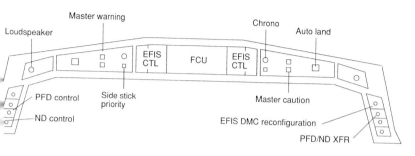

Above: **A340 cockpit glareshield instruments.** *Airbus Industrie*

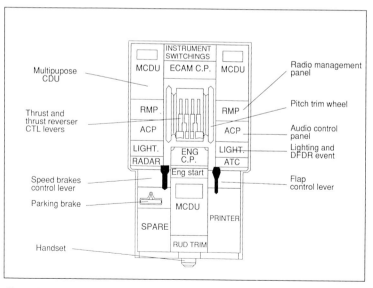

Above: **A340 pedestal instruments.** *Airbus Industrie*

Above: Four A300-600ST Beluga Super Transporters were produced based on the basic A300-600 airframe, with the flightdeck lowered to allow the Airbus airliner family assemblies to be delivered to the final assembly lines at Toulouse and Hamburg by the most efficient method. These aircraft are the largest cargo aircraft in the world and are available for the transportation of any bulky items. *Airbus Industrie*

Left: A wide-body fuselage centre-section arrives at Toulouse from Hamburg aboard the SATIC-produced A300-600ST Beluga Super Transporter. Unloading is now undertaken in a special building to avoid delays due to high winds when the loading hatch is open. *Airbus Industrie*

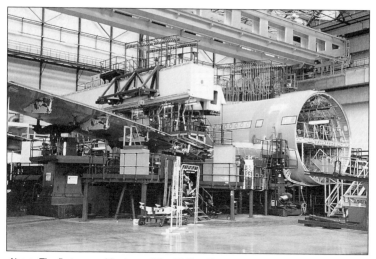

Above: The first assembly stage of the A340 at Toulouse in the specially-built hall is the attachment of the wings to the fuselage using some 3,500 bolts and taking about 35hr over three days. *Author*

Above: The wings are automatically lined up with the fuselage centre-section using computer-controlled lasers. Following the robotic drilling of the holes, the wings are separated to deburr and remove swarf, and then precisely repositioned for the bolts to be put in place. *Airbus Industrie*

Above: The second main assembly stage is the attachment of the front and rear fuselages to the completed wing centre-section, where the composite tail surfaces and the undercarriage units are also attached. The robot-controlled rivet joints of the cabin sections take about 12hr, with the holes drilled and the special rivets assembled, while an operator inside forms the heads. The A340-300 in assembly is MSN 270 for THY (Turk Hava Yollari/Turkish Airlines). *Airbus Industrie*

Above: Once assembled on the undercarriage for the first time, the A330/A340 airframes are moved into an adjacent four-bay hangar, where the pre-assembled systems are connected and further equipment installed. Normally only three bays are in use at a time, with a fourth available for special requirements. MSN N117 in the foreground is an A340-300 which was delivered to SIA in October 1996 as 9V-SJF. *Airbus Industrie*

Above: Once the systems functions are completed, the A330/A340 airframes are moved outside for fuel flows, pressurisation and other checks. The aircraft in the middle of the line is an A340 and the composite tail sections and under-fuselage fairings contrast with the primered metal fuselage and wings. To save costs, the engines are not fitted until after customisation in an adjacent building. *Author*

Left: Once completed, the A340s join the other members of the family on the flight line where they are prepared for flight, production flight tested and offered for customer acceptance and delivery. *Airbus Industrie*

Above: Present at Toulouse at the end of June is A340-300E 9V-SJO, MSN 282, being prepared for flight and carrying the temporary French registration F-WWJX before it achieves the Certificate of Airworthiness and is registered by the new owner. *Author*

Above: A new A340-300 for Air Canada, MSN 278, is carrying the flight test registration C-GDVZ/F-WWJV at Toulouse ready for delivery to the airline on 28 June 1999. *Author*

3. POWERPLANTS

With the powerplants of many modern airliners carried in underwing pods, there is a greater opportunity for providing a choice of engines hung on airframes. This may be considered to give the airlines additional competitiveness but almost always spells economic problems for the engine manufacturer, since it becomes increasingly difficult to achieve a reasonable return on the considerable investment involved in developing the engine and the certification of it on a particular airframe. The most recent example has been the Boeing 777 with the all-new GE90 engine offered by General Electric giving the best development potential, although the derivative engines from Rolls-Royce and Pratt & Whitney, which offer less future development potential, have been produced at a lower cost. As a result, the all-new GE90 engine has attracted less market share and is unlikely to attract high levels of investment to make the most of its potential in future markets. Therefore, the airlines suffer in the long term by not having common engines available for their developing fleets.

The initial versions of the A340 offered only one basic engine: the General Electric/Snecma CFM International CFM56, conceived in the 1960s as a 10-tonne-thrust turbofan, producing nearly 151kN (34,000lb) of thrust. The CFM56-5C for the A340 has a 1.82m diameter fan, which is 10cm wider than the -5A for the A320, and 30cm wider than the -3 fitted to the Boeing 737s. It is designed to develop 151kN thrust, was certificated for up to 145kN, and entered service on the A340 at 140kN. Exhaust gas temperatures at service entry were the same as those of the 111kN -5A, with a modest increase of 25° to achieve 151kN thrust.

The four-stage low-pressure (LP) compressor was completely redesigned for the -5C, including modifications to reduce the susceptibility to rain ingestion, which includes moving the fan/core splitter plate aft to direct more rain outwards into the bypass duct. Hail ingestion was also reduced. The high-pressure (HP) compressor is the same as that used on the CFM56-3 and -5A, with an extra roller bearing behind the main thrust bearing to assist with centring.

Above: The No 1 CFM56-5C4 engine fitted to A340-300E 9V-SJO of SIA has the cowlings open for maintenance access, also showing the high-bypass ducting which reduces noise and increases fuel efficiency. *Author*

The combustor is unchanged, with stage burning used to reduce emissions. All fuel injectors are used at full and mid-power, but at low power only half are operating. Production of nitrogen oxides was more than 40% below ICAO required levels and the engine is expected to meet the anticipated post-2000 emission targets. The full-authority digital engine control (FADEC) is developed from the CFM56-5A with new control laws and electronic technology. The FADEC provides active clearance control of the HP compressor, and the LP and HP turbines. The main shaft with single crystal blades is unchanged from the -5A, but the LP turbine was completely redesigned, adding a fifth stage to drive the larger fan. For the first time a mixed-flow nacelle is used, mixing internally the core and bypass airflows to improve efficiency. CFMI supplies the complete powerplant including the Rohr-built nacelle and the Hispano-built four-door thrust reversers. Weight increase was about 270kg over previous CFM56 powerplants.

The -5C engine has a 5% lower specific fuel consumption than the -5A, and eight engines were allocated to the test programme with initial flight testing on the CFMI 707 testbed. Initial certification was achieved in October 1991, with the higher powered 151kN gaining certification towards the end of 1994. A Garrett-Turbomeca APU supplies enough air to enable the CFM56-5C2 engines to be started in pairs, each side taking less than 1min.

The CFM56-5C was the highest thrust of the type likely to be developed, although developments continued for a number of other Airbus single-aisle airliners. Therefore, any significant improvements to the A340 requiring more power would have to use a new engine, losing any commonality for airlines operating both earlier and later types, but commonality would remain with the narrow-bodied fleets.

As a result, in May 1991 Airbus confirmed that new engines would be required for future versions of the A340, and Rolls-Royce considered an advanced derivative of the RB.211-535 with a thrust in excess of 180kN (40,000lb), offering a potential alternative engine for the planned stretched A321 and developments of the Boeing 757. The first A340 was powered by four 137.5kN CFM56-5C2 engines and although these engines

could power developed versions, new engines would allow the higher gross weight and stretched A340-200X, -300X and -400X to have an increased range. The new engine required a thrust range of 156kN to 200kN and Pratt & Whitney was studying a 160kN version of its PW2000, known as the PW2136. The General Electric GE90 was seen as too large for the A340 application, but the technology of this new engine could be desirable in a smaller version. Not surprisingly, CFMI announced that it was also considering the development of a new engine, its 50/50 partnership with GE bringing the potential of new GE90 technology. The anticipated market for the A340 was seen as 270 aircraft, with many powered by the CFM engines, so whatever engine was selected would need additional applications to justify development.

In mid-1993, International Aero Engines (IAE) announced plans to develop an ultra-high-bypass ducted fan engine, based on the core of the V2500, with growth versions of the A340 as the target. The planned power would be between 178kN and 190kN (40,000lb to 42,000lb) thrust, and the engine would have a bypass ratio of between 14:1 and 15:1. By the middle of 1995 there were four engines on offer for the developed versions of the A340, the options under study being the Rolls-Royce RB211-411, the P&W PW2143, P&W's Advanced Ducted Prop (ADP), and the yet-to-be-launched CFM XX. The ADP was seen as an unlikely contender due to the high costs, and the selected engine manufacturers would be expected to invest in the non-recurring costs of the re-engining programme.

Towards the end of 1995, the selection appeared to have narrowed to a choice between the CFMI partners Snecma, General Electric and Pratt & Whitney to secure an exclusive agreement to provide the powerplant for the developed versions of the A340. CFMI proposed the new 178-200kN thrust CFM XX and Pratt & Whitney was offering the 191-200kN variant of the PW2040. Not unexpectedly, with a restricted market for the stretched A340 carrying a further 50 passengers, the $2 billion development costs could only justify an exclusive engine supplier.

In April 1996, GE and Airbus signed an exclusive agreement to power what had by then become the stretched 375-passenger, 13,000km

Above: Emphasising the family of Airbus airliners at the Paris Show in June 1999, a fly-past was made of all the types in production for the first time, highlighting the first 30 years of Airbus success. The formation was led by the A319 Corporate Jetliner, followed by the single-aisle A320 in Sichuan Airlines colours, and an Iberian A321 with test registration D-AVZL. The twin-aisle wide-bodies consist of A310-300, D-AIDM, Egyptair A300-600, SU-GAR, Gulf Air A330-200, F-WWKI, the A340-300 No 1, and, nosing in from the left, one of the four A300-600ST Belugas. *Airbus Industrie*

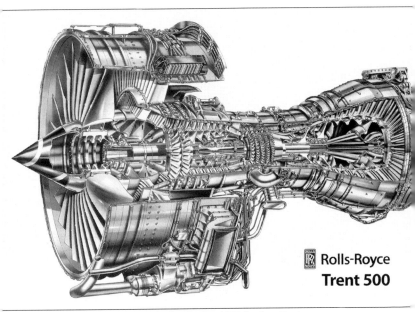

Rolls-Royce
Trent 500

Above: Rolls-Royce is developing the Trent 500 for the ultra-long-range A340-500/600 programme. With a take-off thrust of 56,000lb the first engine will be flight tested on the Airbus-owned No 1 A340-300 test-bed under one of the inboard wing pylons in 2000, with certification due by the end of the year. Rolls-Royce is currently the sole engine supplier for the ultra-long-range A340 family, but competition may come from Pratt & Whitney. *Rolls-Royce*

(7,000nm) A340-600. GE had been involved with Airbus from the start with the CF6 engines on the A300, and the agreement covered the development of a new, or derivative, engine in the 227kN (51,000lb) thrust class. The derivative engine could be a development of the CF6, incorporating GE90 technology.

Snecma, GE's partner in CFMI, had wanted to lead the CFM XX engine proposed jointly with the development of the hot-section, but this was unacceptable to GE, even though the existing agreement prohibited Snecma from working on a competitive cold-section, effectively stopping that programme. There was also disagreement between Snecma and Airbus over the pricing of the existing CFM56-5s for the A340, making it difficult for Airbus to compete with the Boeing 777 due to cut-throat competition between the three

engine manufacturers. However, the situation improved in August 1996 with a change of senior management at Snecma, bringing the company back into contact with GE, the derivative engine being the most likely solution.

The exclusivity agreement between Airbus and GE was valid for six months, leaving open the options for Rolls-Royce or P&W to re-enter negotiations if agreement with GE was not reached. Despite running past the original deadline, negotiations continued into December 1996, by then centred around a new engine involving a 401mm-diameter fan yielding a very high bypass of 9.4, with thrust between 240 and 270kN (55,000 and 60,000lb). With a number of other programme decisions to be made, including a growth version of the GE90 for the Boeing 777, GE had significant economic issues to consider, especially as margins in many cases were virtually non-existent. As a result of difficulties with agreement on price and risk-sharing, GE decided to pull out of the talks with Airbus in early 1997, as with only one potential airframe application there would not be a satisfactory return on the estimated $1 billion costs of developing a new engine.

Meanwhile, Rolls-Royce had continued to study the 245-290kN (55,000-65,000lb) thrust Trent developments using a scaled down Trent 800 core and the fan from the Trent 700. In addition to being applicable to the A340 developments, it had a potential second application in the planned Boeing 767-400ERX. As the derivative engine would make extensive use of existing technology, the business case was expected to be more attractive. By March 1997 Snecma was also in discussion with Rolls-Royce for a share in the proposed engine.

With the collapse of the GE negotiations, Airbus restarted talks with both Rolls-Royce and Pratt & Whitney with the aim of achieving a launch decision in mid-1997, both engine manufacturers offering derivative engines. The two powerplants on offer were the R-R Trent 500 and the P&W PW4557 which were very closely matched on paper, but both manufacturers were insisting on an exclusive engine deal to avoid the price cutting demanded by the airlines.

However, at the Paris Show in June 1997, Airbus and Rolls-Royce came to a non-exclusive agreement for the supply of the Trent 500 engines for the A340, and although Pratt & Whitney could still offer its PW4000 derivative, it was thought unlikely due to the business case. The Trent 500 was a 250kN (56,000lb) thrust derivative of the Trent 700 as fitted to the A330 and the Trent 800 as fitted to the Boeing 777. The fan diameter was reduced and a new low-pressure turbine fitted. Growth potential was expected to be to 275kN, and fuel consumption was 7.7% better than the Trent 700. The first run of the Trent 500 was scheduled for the second quarter of 1999 and flight testing was planned for 2000 with a Trent installed in place of one of the existing CFM56s on the A340-300 prototype. Certification of the engine is planned for the end of 2000, with the first A340-600 flying in early 2001 powered by the new Trent 500 engines.

Above: **The No 1 and No 2 CFM56-5 engines fitted to the first A340-300 during the flight development programme.**
Airbus Industrie

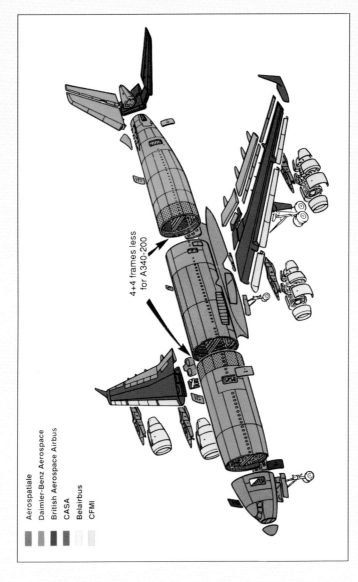

Aerospatiale
Daimler-Benz Aerospace
British Aerospace Airbus
CASA
Belairbus
CFMI

4+4 frames less
for A340-200

Above: The A340 design and production responsibility was shared out amongst the partners in a similar way to the earlier airliners, with the major assemblies arriving at Toulouse from all over Europe. *Airbus Industrie*

Above: The lower NC-machined wing skins for the A340 feature cut-outs for access to the integral fuel tanks. The thickness is checked by ultra-sonics and the machine marks are removed by bead blasting, which also relieves any stresses. *BAe Airbus*

Left: The wing spars, ribs and leading edge ribs are all machined for greater precision and ease of assembly. The wing skins have the stringers attached automatically by Drivmatic riveting. The wings are assembled and inspected in vertical jigs with the leading edge upward. *BAe Airbus*

4. FLIGHT DEVELOPMENT

Major assembly of the first A340 began in late November 1990 at the new Clement Ader facility at Toulouse with the arrival of the first fuselage sections from the Aérospatiale Saint Nazaire plant, flown in by Super Guppy. The first load was the 21m-long forward fuselage, the front section of which was produced by Deutsche Airbus, plus a 16m-long centre-section, to be mated with the British-built wings. In January the Deutsche Airbus-built rear fuselage, the tailplane from CASA in Spain, and engine pylons from Aérospatiale at Toulouse all arrived for assembly.

Production of the A330/A340 programme is international. The cockpit and forward under-fuselage are built by Aérospatiale, Canadair produces major structural parts of the wing centre-section, Aerospace Technologies of Australia (ASTA) makes the floor support structure and the pressure bulkhead between the passenger cabin and the main undercarriage compartment and Hawker de Havilland in Australia manufactures the

wingtip devices and some other parts. The Australian and Canadian companies are risk-sharing partners in the programme, with responsibility for design and development for their share of the programme. Upper fuselage sections over the wing centre-section were produced in Yugoslavia, and forward upper structures come from South Korea.

Assembly of the first aircraft commenced at Workstation 35 early in 1991, with an initial planned rate of one aircraft per month, ready to move up to four per month. With the arrival of new assembly tooling, production rates of seven aircraft were planned from 1994. The British Aerospace-built wings were assembled to the centre fuselage by the end of January 1991, the joining being controlled by computer, involving aligning the wing, and then drilling the 3,500 attachment bolt holes. The completed wing and fuselage centre-section was then moved to an adjacent position for the next stage.

Above: The first A340-300, F-WWAI, when structurally complete and with CFM56 engines fitted was rolled out of the Toulouse final assembly hall at the end of May 1991 for fuel flow and pressure tests before painting and preparation for flight. *Airbus Industrie*

Above: F-WWAI made the maiden flight from Toulouse on 25 October 1991. The lower trailing pair of wheels on the wing-mounted main undercarriage are held in this position by hydraulics to give the effect of a taller undercarriage to avoid tail-strike, but take up less room when retracted. *BAe Airbus*

Robotics are used to control the semi-automatic riveting system for the joining of the front, centre and rear sections of the fuselage. The robotic machine drills a hole, injects sealant and puts a rivet in place. A worker inside the fuselage then forms the head on the rivet before the machine moves on to the next hole, a total of 13,000 rivets being used to join the three fuselage sections. During March, the fin, tailplane, engine pylons and undercarriage were fitted, although with full production established, this process now takes three days. At the end of March, the first A340 moved to one of three docks for the installation of the CFM56-5C2 engines and system testing was completed. All the flight test recording equipment was also fitted, ready for the busy flight development programme.

Roll-out of the first A340, the seventh new type of the Airbus family, was at Toulouse on 4 October 1991. At the same time an order from Korean Air was announced for seven A330s, with options on a further eight. The prototype A340 was then prepared with full systems checks, engine runs and taxi tests ready for the maiden flight on 25 October with chief test pilot Pierre Baud in command. During this first flight of 4hr 47min most of the normal flight envelope was examined, the aircraft handling similarly to the A320, which

was achieved by the fly-by-wire flight-control systems in both types. On this first flight, the A340 reached the maximum operating speed of 335kt (620km/h), flew to an altitude of 40,000ft (12,100m), and the minimum speed was 120kt. At 200 tonnes, the take-off weight was only 53.3 tonnes below the maximum, and equivalent to that required for a transatlantic operation. A total of six A340s participated in the flight development programme which lasted 2,000hr over a period of 14 months. Some of the work

Above: On the maiden flight the A340 was operated by a multinational team of five crew. In command was Pierre Baud, VP Flight Division and chief test pilot in the left-hand seat, assisted by Nick Warner. *Airbus Industrie*

Above: With the staging folded back and the attachments removed, the A340 wings are slid out on a special track. *BAe Airbus*

Above: The joint A330/A340 static test airframe successfully withstood the maximum load anticipated in a lifetime of service in a test which resulted in the wingtips being bent up by 13ft 2in/4.02m in the massive test rig. This was used as a practical check of the design calculations and paved the way for the first flight. *Aérospatiale*

Above: All the current versions of the A340 are powered by four CFM56-5C2 or -5C4 high-bypass fan engines, providing unrestricted operation over long-haul oceanic routes. *Airbus Industrie*

Above: The four wing pylon-mounted CFM56-5C engines which power the A340 are fully accessible for routine maintenance. *Airbus Industrie*

was applicable to the twin A330, particularly in the area of systems reliability, to help achieve an early extended-range operations (Erops) clearance, previously known as ETOPS or extended-range twin-engined operations.

Four of the six test aircraft were A340-300s, the first two being comprehensively equipped with 9 tonnes of measuring, recording and telemetry equipment, capable of recording up to 20,000 parameters, as was done with the first example of the A340-200. The three instrumented aircraft carried out the bulk of the flight trials, opening up the flight envelope and verifying performance on take-off, cruise and landing. The remaining two A340-300s and the A340-200 were equipped with light instrumentation together with full passenger cabins containing seats, toilets and galleys. These aircraft were allocated to test cabin development and environmental control, to verify autopilot behaviour and finally for route-proving.

As with all Airbus aircraft, the A340 flight trials were carried out by the consortium's own test pilots, with Aérospatiale providing the on-board instrumentation, monitoring the telemetry and processing the results. Airbus Industrie makes extensive use of telemetry for routine measurement, in addition to critical tests, to speed

Above: The cabin of the No 1 A340 is heavily instrumented and retained by Airbus Industrie for continuing flight development. On the maiden flight the flight test equipment was monitored by Gerard Guyot, on the left, and Jürgen Hammer, and heavy use is made of telemetry on all test flying to obtain results in real time. When milestones have been reached, authority can be given to move on to the next stage without having to return and land. This saves considerably on flight test time and costs, and increases efficiency. *Airbus Industrie*

Above: A critical test is the Vr (Velocity rotation) to ensure that with the tail, protected by a wooden skid, scraping the runway, the aircraft will still become safely airborne without stalling, as is demonstrated by A340-300 F-WWAI with the extended main wheel undercarriage just clear of the ground. *Airbus Industrie*

Above: Another critical, and often spectacular, test is the maximum energy stop. This is at a high all-up weight and usually blows all the tyres, but is necessary to show that any excess heat is safely contained. *Airbus Industrie*

the processing of results, allowing the test programme to be developed during flight. With the addition of a second control room at Toulouse, two aircraft could be handled simultaneously. The first A340 has been retained as a development testbed, with the other five being refurbished and put into airline service.

By the end of November the A340 had achieved speeds from as low as 100kt (185km/h) at low altitude, to Mach 0.85 at 40,000ft (12,200m). The aircraft had been flown at all three take-off configurations and achieved a take-off weight of 230 tonnes, 23.5 tonnes below the maximum. By the end of December, the 100hr flight mark had been passed, with 63hr being achieved in December. The seven Airbus pilots who had flown the aircraft confirmed it had similar handling to the smaller A320. System reliability was already at levels required for commercial service. Stalling had been cleared, flutter trials had started and handling had been tested at the extremes of the centre of gravity. The CFM56-5C2 engines had been cleared to a higher thrust rating of 145kN (32,500lb). The second A340-311 joined the flight development programme on 3 February 1992.

During the early flight testing, it was revealed to the customer airlines that the range was 1% below the levels guaranteed, but that a modification to improve performance had been incorporated and shown to work. At the same airline briefing it was confirmed that the aircraft was within the weight specifications and on time with the production and certification schedule. As a result of various

modifications to the wing, Airbus was confident that the range guarantees would be beaten by 4% on service entry in January 1993. About one third was recovered by increasing the chord of the inboard slats by 10%, and the balance came from improvements to the engines and minor changes in rigging and sealing.

The performance and reliability of the engines was on target, wing performance in low and high-speed flight had been confirmed and the systems reliability was as good as on a mature aircraft. During flight testing an unexpectedly severe buffet had been experienced at low lift coefficients caused by flow separation. This was cured by a large metal fairing inboard of the outer engine, which could be removed for access to the wing but was later deleted. It was also found at an early stage that the nose undercarriage leg may have been too short, giving the aircraft a nose-down attitude and leaving the rear cargo and passenger doors 37cm too high. The nose leg was lengthened by 41cm, but as the new version was not ready for service introduction, the interim solution was to add an onboard airstair for the passenger doors, and a special cargo handling system to make the aircraft compatible with existing cargo loading systems. Handling qualities were enhanced mainly by improving speed brake and spoiler buffet, and the outer ailerons were inhibited in the cruise to prevent excessive wing response.

During February 1992 a flight was made to Singapore taking 13hr, which was the longest duration to date, in which the cockpit proved

Above: A total of six A340s were used in the flight development programme leading to certification. In addition to the first A340-300, F-WWAI, the first A340-200, F-WWBA, was also heavily instrumented and is seen flying nearest to the camera aircraft. *Airbus Industrie*

Above: As part of the checking of the inertial navigation equipment, F-WWAI became the first Airbus to fly over the North Pole in August 1992. The rather desolate region can be seen in front of the No 3 CFM56 engine. *Airbus Industrie*

Above: As well as demonstrating its capabilities in warm and temperate climates, the A340-211 F-WWBA undertook cold weather trials at Kiruna in Sweden during December 1992. Here the aircraft undergoes a cold-soak to ensure all the systems will function in extreme cold. *Airbus Industrie*

Above: Operating from the Paris Air Show, A340-211 F-WWBA completed a World Ranger flight over Asia to Auckland, departing on 16 June 1993. It returned to Paris on 18 June, flying over Alaska and Greenland. The nonstop distance to Auckland of 10,310nm/19,100km took exactly 21hr 32min. The return flight of 10,392 nm/19,258 km took a further 21hr 46min. *Airbus Industrie*

Above: Quite early in the flight trials, the A340 was showing such excellent reliability that it was able to make a number of overseas flights, both as part of the trials and to demonstrate the aircraft to prospective customers, although the cabin was not furnished. In July 1992 aircraft No 1 visited Jeddah. *Airbus Industrie*

extremely comfortable. The third aircraft joined the flight test programme on 1 April, and was the first of the longer-range A340-200s, the high systems reliability having allowed testing to exceed 375hr in 86 flights. The wing drag and buffet modifications were installed on the second A340 at the British Aerospace plant at Filton at the end of April. On 15 June the third A340-311 joined the test fleet, followed by the second A340-211 on 20 July and the fourth A340-311 on 31 July. The second -211 was eventually delivered to Lufthansa as D-AIBF and the fourth -311 to Air France as F-GLZA. By September the six test aircraft had flown more than 1,200hr and completed all the basic safety and performance trials.

As part of the range guarantee requirement, Airbus started testing an engine performance improvement package (PIP) in August to provide a 1.5% improvement in fuel consumption before service entry and a further 1% later on. The engine modifications included new combustion chambers to improve fuel burn, and the rerouteing of cooling flow through the turbine to improve engine cooling.

More aerodynamic improvements were being studied during October 1992 to further fine tune the airframe and improve the range. A fillet fairing was tried on the outboard engine pylons to reduce

Above: In October 1992 A340-300 F-WWAI flew as far as Melbourne in Australia. *Airbus Industrie*

Above: Early in the flight development programme, A340-211 D-AIBF for Lufthansa operated at La Paz, Bolivia, one of the highest airports in the world, demonstrating its landing and take-off performance in the rarefied air. *Airbus Industrie*

interference drag. The outboard pylons required more attention than the inboard, perhaps because this was the first four-engined airliner by Airbus. Other options included the change of contour of the leading edge slats. The final decision on any of the modifications depended on the cost-effectiveness of the results. The most demanding range case was for Singapore Airlines, who had selected the A340 after abandoning MD-11s when they could not meet the payload/range targets for the nonstop Singapore to Paris route. SIA wanted to operate the higher-gross-weight version of the A340 with a guaranteed payload of 28.6 tonnes on the Singapore-Paris service.

Although the flight development programme covered a wide range of activities, the payload/range performance is always of greatest interest to the airlines. However, another improvement was that the empty weight was about 500kg better than expected, the total empty weight

Above: With Singapore Airlines a strong prospect, A340-311 F-WWDA visited Singapore in November 1992. *Airbus Industrie*

Above: In October 1996, the A340-300 No 1 F-WWAI clearly demonstrated that it could handle without difficulty the demanding conditions at Lhasa, which at an altitude of 3,570m, is one of the world's highest airports. It has the additional hazard of being surrounded on three sides by mountains and the A340 was also able to demonstrate its ability to make a three-engine ferry flight from this restricted location. *Airbus Industrie*

Above: Amongst the launch customers for the A340 were Air France and Lufthansa, who had been loyal supporters of the product line from the start of the A300. Air France A340-300 F-WWCA is seen on a pre-delivery test flight. *Airbus Industrie*

Above: Lufthansa placed initial orders for six of the shorter long-range A340-211s, D-AIBA flying near the Pyrenees before becoming the first aircraft delivered to the airline on 29 January 1993. *Airbus Industrie*

Above: Also a consistent supporter of Airbus from the early days is Iberia, who placed an early order for eight A340-300s with options on a further four. A340-300 EC-154 is seen on a pre-delivery test flight before adopting its permanent registration. *Airbus Industrie*

Above: **A340-300 No 1, F-WWAI, undertook cold weather trials in Yakutsk (Republic of Sakha) where the sun barely rises during the short winter days.** *Airbus Industrie*

of the A340-200 being in the order of 118.5 tonnes. This allowed the fuel capacity to be increased by 3,600 litres using extra tankage in the wings. The take-off performance was improved, the maximum gross take-off weight (MTOW) being raised from the original 253.5 tonnes to around 257 tonnes. This allowed the airlines to carry more payload/fuel options, benefiting the long-range operations. Clmax (lift coefficient) was better than expected, and early results from the tests revealed a 1% drag reduction and a 1.5% improvement in fuel burn. Further drag reductions were achieved by the use of riblets pioneered by Airbus and 3M. These consist of clear plastic film with fine strakes and

were attached to the upper wing surface, tailplane, fuselage and the entire fin. Both the first A340s for Lufthansa and Air France were fitted with this film for evaluation during the first year of operation, the expected gain being about 0.7% extra range. Other modifications being considered were rear-fuselage strakes and an increase in the outboard wing incidence, the latter being more expensive but giving up to 1% more range. The rear-fuselage strakes were expected to give a 0.5% range improvement. Each one in itself appeared a modest gain, but the combination on the long distances involved could make the difference between achieving and not achieving a particular route with a profitable payload.

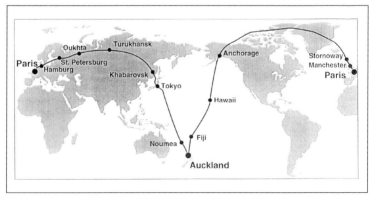

Above: **Airbus A340 World Ranger route map.** *Airbus Industrie*

Above: The cabin of the A340-211, F-WWBA, used for the World Ranger flight to Auckland was rather basically furnished for the 43hr 18min in the air, and total elapsed time of 48hr 22 min. *Airbus Industrie*

Another challenge for Airbus, only made possible with fly-by-wire flying controls, was to make the A340 cross-operable with the A330, so that airlines with both types would have reduced crew training costs. Additionally, as the flightdeck and fly-by-wire system were developed from the much smaller A320, crew compatibility could also be achieved.

Before take-off in the A340, the zero fuel weight, centre of gravity position and runway speeds are entered manually. On the primary flight display (PFD) the initial climb safety speed (V2) and the decision speed (V1) are displayed. Cockpit preparation is brief and is done by pressing all system switches which show white. All the circuit breakers are located below the floor, but their status can be checked on the electronic centralised aircraft monitor (ECAM). Any one of three display management computers, each with segregated electronic flight instrument system and ECAM channels, can drive all six displays in four formats. Either navigation display (ND) can display ECAM systems, and the PFD can interchange with the ND. Other computing is selected from three switches on the head of the pedestal. Air data and inertial reference or audio control can be fed by a third system, and either flight management computer 1 or 2 feeds to both display units. The flight management system (FMS) is similar to the

A320, but adds fuel-dump and point-of-no-return prediction capability for long flights. A vertical mode, determining climb speeds and altitude for climb power selection, was added later.

Flight control movements are checked on the configuration display, which also shows the status of the flight control computers. Before take-off, check items are scanned quickly, with only some six items needing pilot confirmation. From cockpit entry to take-off, the systems handle most of the checks. Although the flap and slat angles vary, the references are the same as on the A320, and on the airspeed scale, F and S markers indicate when to retract flaps and slats. The pitch trim automatically compensates for all configuration changes, as well as for the speed. If a spoiler panel fails, the opposite panel ceases to operate, and if the rudder yaw-damping is lost, the spoilers operate in pairs to compensate. The auto-throttle automatically applies go-around power at 'Alpha floor' angle, and 'Alpha max' is the ultimate angle achievable with full rearward control input, which is just below the angle of maximum lift coefficient. At stall warning speed the nose pitches down on stick release, then as the speed increases again, it reverts to the normal pitch law. Automatic flight control is limited to 305kt and M0.80, and is advised on the ECAM. If all three inertial reference systems were to fail, a no-feedback link to the

51

Above: Turk Hava Yollari/Turkish Airlines placed an initial order for five A340-311s, later increasing to seven. Its first aircraft, TC-JDJ, first flew on 23 June 1993 and was delivered to THY on 10 August. *Airbus Industrie*

Above: TAP Air Portugal initially ordered two A340-311s, but later added two more. A340-311 CS-TOA is seen on a test flight and was delivered to TAP on 22 December 1994, together with the second aircraft, CS-TOB. *Airbus Industrie*

Above: Gulf Air ordered six A340-300s with options on six more in September 1992, but due to over-capacity a number were leased to other operators for various periods. The first A340-312, A40-LA, seen taking off from Toulouse with French test registration F-WWJX, was leased to Philippine Airlines and then went to Sabena. *Airbus Industrie*

Above: In August 1997 Olympic Airways became a new customer for the A340 with an order for two aircraft, plus options on two more. The first two A340-313s, SX-DFA and SX-DFB, were delivered to the airline on 29 January 1999. SX-DFB, named Delphi, is seen on a pre-delivery test flight. The two options were confirmed in early 1999. *Airbus Industrie*

control surfaces results, and no-stability augmentation is required. In the full natural stall, the warning operates and at 24° the nose drops automatically, even with full-back stick, and wings remain level 5°. Mechanical reversion, with direct control of rudder and pitch trim, is available if all else fails. On final approach flare initiation is at 30ft, and if a reverser fails to operate, the matching reverser on the other wing is blocked from operation. Engine retard is warned orally at 20ft, and when the power levers are pulled to idle, the auto-thrust disengages.

Although the A340 cockpit is fitted with four thrust levers, compared with the A320 and A330 which have only two, nearly all the other features are indistinguishable in the air, despite the weight of the A340 being 3.5 times as much as the A320. Conversion on all three types is achievable within 10 days, compared with a normal two-month conversion programme. Not only are crew training costs drastically reduced with pilots rated on a

Above: In August 1995, A340-300 F-WWAI made a perfect automatic landing at Mmbatho, near Johannesburg, using the differential global positioning system (DGPS) based on satellite navigation.
Airbus Industrie

number of types, but airlines gain greater flexibility of crew rostering. The system is known as cross-crew qualification (CCQ), which allows a pilot to have a full type-rating on one aircraft within a group of aircraft which are ruled to be generically similar (but not sufficiently similar for a common type-rating), then being able to gain full ratings on others with a shortened type-rating course. This then allows mixed fleet operations.

In mid-November the Lufthansa A340-200 and Air France A340-300 test aircraft were put on a combined route-proving and certification programme, a further modification required by the FAA being additional projection of the fuel tanks in the unlikely event of an uncontained engine failure.

During the route-proving programme with the Lufthansa A340, it was appreciated that from the passenger's point of view, there were a number of advances that made long-distance flights more pleasant. Lufthansa had suggested over 400 ideas for improving passenger comfort, more than half of which were adopted. With four engines, the A340 does not need the 50% of extra power required with all twin-engined airliners to allow for an engine failure on take-off. The A340 passengers therefore do not experience the high runway acceleration and vigorous rotation of the twin during take-off, giving the aircraft the feel of a long-range airliner. During the take-off roll, as the wings take the load, the tips can be seen to rise through several feet, to lift the aircraft at weights of up to 257,000kg, and the long ascent to cruise altitude is a long-range characteristic reminiscent of the Boeing 747.

One of the most noticeable improvements experienced by the passengers was the quietness of the cabin, mainly achieved by the new air-conditioning system, designed for quieter operation. Another improvement of the air-conditioning system requested by Lufthansa, and adopted with the fleet, was to split the system into six temperature-independent sections along the cabin. This is intended to keep the passengers in the rear cabin from freezing when the temperature adjusts automatically for the heat produced when food is served in the first and business class cabins. Apart from some problems with the air-conditioning system early on in the route-proving operations, the trials were virtually trouble-free. There were no mechanical failures to systems, airframe or engines, and no major black boxes needed changing on either of the two route-proving A340s. The Lufthansa A340-200 was fitted with 3 tonnes of test equipment in the rear cabin, monitored throughout by flight test engineers.

During route-proving the ride comfort was found to be very good, an example being when moderate clear-air turbulence was encountered, the cabin crew were able to continue service when normally they would have been forced to stop. There is also a higher standard of seating than on other Lufthansa long-range aircraft, with seats limited to six abreast in business class, equivalent to first class a few years previously. The first and business class passengers are provided with 12-channel personal video systems folding out of the seat arm as part of the flight entertainment system, while economy passengers have eight channels of compact disc sound to choose from.

One benefit from the route-proving was that the 1.5° nose-down attitude of the aircraft on the ground did not interfere with ground-handling operations. Pallets and containers were loaded at several locations without difficulty. Access stairs were found to reach the rear passenger door sills without any difficulty, giving Airbus less urgency for introducing the new longer nosewheel leg.

During the trials, the Lufthansa aircraft operated 40 flights consisting of a total of 141hr 25min flying time. Nearly 100,000km (54,000nm) were flown, the longest leg being nonstop from Frankfurt to Honolulu, a distance of 12,300km in a time of 15hr 20min. Air France flew the A340-300 on 29 flights with a total airborne time of 140hr 45min, the longest operation being from Singapore to Paris, covering 11,500km in 14hr 30min. An A340-200 on routine flight testing flew from Toulouse to Perth, Western Australia, with a 27-tonne payload in 16hr 22min and arrived with nearly 4hr of fuel remaining.

The A340 met its guaranteed range of 12,800km with a full load of passengers, although the longest range to be flown initially was the 10,000km from Frankfurt to São Paulo and fuel burn was about 30% less than a similarly loaded DC-10. With low-speed performance better than predicted, the take-off weight was increased by up to 3.5 tonnes to 257 tonnes for the same power. The addition of nacelle strakes helped reduce the A340-300 approach speed by around 8kt (15km/h).

The series of worldwide route-proving flights undertaken by Lufthansa and Air France was probably more wide-ranging and comprehensive than before, and followed the extensive flight test programme carried out by Airbus.

European certification was awarded for both the A340-200 and -300 on 22 December 1992 by 18 European joint airworthiness authorities (JAA), ready for delivery and service entry with Air France and Lufthansa in March 1993, followed by FAA certification on 27 May. In June 1993, an A340-200 broke the record for the longest nonstop flight by an airliner, when it was flown on a World Ranger operation from the Paris Air Show at Le Bourget to Auckland in New Zealand. With chief test pilot Pierre Baud leading a crew of five and a further 15 occupants, the departure from Le Bourget was at 11.58hrs local time on 16 June. The distance covered was 19,100km (10,310nm) in an elapsed time of 21hr 32min, arriving at Auckland at 19.30hrs local time on 17 June —

Above: On final approach to land, the A340 shows the full-span leading edge slats, and the trailing edge flaps supplemented by the aileron droop. *Airbus Industrie*

Above: The first A340 to be delivered was A340-211 D-AIBA which went to Lufthansa on 2 February 1993. With Lufthansa now being part of the Star Alliance, this aircraft has been painted in the identities of Lufthansa, SAS, Thai, Varig, Air Canada and United. *Lufthansa/Dietmar Plath*

Above: Lufthansa A340-211 D-AIBA after push-back at Munich airport. *Lufthansa/Dr Werner Henni*

Above: In February 1993 Virgin Atlantic signed a letter of intent for four A340s to develop the route structure to the USA, Asia and South Africa. A340-311 G-VBUS was delivered on 26 November 1993. *Airbus Industrie*

Above: The first A340-311, F-GLZB, was handed over to Air France on 26 February 1993 and was the 1,000th Airbus airliner to be delivered, the first A300B4 having been delivered to Air France in May 1974. The next 1,000 Airbus airliners should be delivered in less than 19 years, with a current average of an airliner delivered every day. The aircraft is seen departing from Toulouse on the delivery flight. *Airbus Industrie*

25min ahead of schedule with 14.6 tonnes of fuel remaining. The return was made to Le Bourget on 18 June.

Following certification, development flying continued to improve performance, particularly with regard to a further reduction in drag and an increase in engine efficiency to maximise the range. New equipment tested included a heads-down enhanced vision system (EVS) with an infra-red camera mounted on the nose gear leg. The forward-looking image can be selected by the captain on the navigation display screen. Although all the Airbus family have full automatic landing, the infra-red system could assist during low-visibility taxying, runway lining up and ensuring that the runway is clear for take-off. It also permits reduced minima for automatic landings on runways with ILS but lacking the specified lighting standards for Category III landings. The camera installation was tested on dedicated taxying trials, and on approaches during other test flying.

The early in-service experience with the four-engined A340 was used to achieve earlier approval of extended-range twinjet operations with the A330. Airbus Industrie and the A340 launch airlines, Air France and Lufthansa, operated a 13-month programme to analyse the operational performance and reliability of the key airframe systems common to both types. The programme monitored some 4,000 operating cycles over a period of nearly 15,000 flying hours, experience having shown that most in-flight engine shutdowns and diversions have been systems-related rather than propulsion failures. The most critical Erops-related equipment on the A330, such as the fuel and maintenance computers, and hydraulics and electrical systems, are common to both types and therefore could be validated cost-effectively on the A340s in service. With every A340 flight of over 6hr duration, the minimum equipment list was monitored before departure, and recorded whether dispatch would have been allowed under Erops rules. While in the air, any equipment malfunction or systems warnings were logged and later analysed to determine the consequences had they occurred on an Erops operation. Some Erops specific testing was also undertaken, an example being starting the APU 30min before the descent, after a long cold-soak, and diversion procedures were demonstrated by

simulating various systems failures during a North Atlantic flight. During the first three months of the programme, events were registered on 2% of the flights, examples being spurious warnings with the flight management computer, and a faulty flow-control valve on an air-conditioning pack. This work not only helped to make the A330 more Erops compliant, but also improved the reliability of the A340 systems, fulfilling the Erops principle in both twin and four-engined aircraft.

Airbus Industrie also achieved a milestone when the A340 became the first in-service large airliner to be navigated by a global positioning system (GPS), when the Litton system was certificated at the end of 1993, to be followed by a Honeywell GPS later. Although the airlines were keen to install the equipment there was no operational credit for using the system, but some of the destinations served by the A340 were lacking suitable aids, and the GPS would help with positioning. Neither the JAA nor the FAA allows sole-use GPS navigation at present, since they will not have remote autonomous integrity monitoring which will be required for sole-means GPS navigation. The certification was therefore for the GPS to be used as a supplemental aid. In practice, the pilot in a GPS-equipped A340 would see the position appear on the navigation display, which might be either GPS, inertial navigation system or beacon derived. The way the pilot could find out which system is providing the information is by calling up another page on cockpit display. The GPS is so accurate that it would be the most likely navigation source used, but it could be deselected by the pilot if necessary.

In August 1994, the US FAA joined the European JAA in certificating the new Airbus CCQ, allowing pilots to hold common type-ratings on all Airbus types from the A320 onwards. This was made possible by the high degree of commonality between the fly-by-wire A320, A321, A330 and A340, with the virtually identical cockpits and systems, as well as similar handling characteristics, despite the differences in size. Although CCQ is an Airbus term, the principle was first accepted on the Boeing 757 and 767, but the acceptance of the Airbus CCQ was more demanding due to the twin-engined and four-engined variations, as well as being narrow-body and wide-body aircraft with significant differences

Above: Airbus A340-300 test-bed F-WWAI continues in use with Airbus Industrie to help with the flight testing of new innovations, particularly the pre-development of the A340-500/600. *Airbus Industrie*

in gross weight. The CCQ permits a pilot qualified to fly the A320 to convert to the A321 by completing one day of conversion training covering the differences. The conversion from the twin-engined narrow-body A320 to the four-engine wide-body A340 normally takes just a few days.

In 1998 Airbus introduced a variety of new automated functions to improve the safety of the A340 and all other new production aircraft. The initiatives, coupled with improved pilot feedback and training, were designed to reduce the number of human error incidents, which are believed to account for 70% of all jet airliner accidents. It was estimated that if all the first and second-generation turbine-powered aircraft were replaced by the newer automated types, the global accident rates could be cut by a factor of two. Most accidents fall into four main categories: controlled flight into terrain (CFT), loss of control, undershooting the runway, and running off the end of a runway either on take-off or landing. New technology can assist the pilots in saving their passengers, but it must be remembered that few accidents are classed as simply crew error, since the operating environment is always a factor and affects the actions of the crew.

The new automated functions included assistance for the pilots of the abort/continue decision following an emergency during take-off, where 20% of the accidents occur. An acceleration monitoring system is linked to the critical rotation speed and the amount of runway remaining, as pilots tend to be more likely to abort the departure, which in practice is often more critical, than continuing the take-off. A revised take-off pitch-control law was introduced to prevent over-rotation and tailstrike. The already mentioned GPS system became standard, allowing accurate and safe instrument approaches down to 250ft (75m) above the ground. Differential GPS (DGPS) will eventually replace current precision approach aids, allowing it to become a stand-alone prime system for navigation. Enhanced ground-proximity warning systems (EGPWS) is fitted as standard, providing 30sec warning of an obstacle, compared with the 10sec of existing GPWS. The EGWPS and GPS will be integrated to provide an automatic escape manoeuvre function in the flight control system to be considered. This would initiate an automatic go-around if all alerts are ignored.

The continued use of advanced technology and product development keeps Airbus Industrie competitive in the world markets, providing the airlines with a continued choice of major airliner manufacturers.

Above: By autumn 1993 Sabena had introduced the A340-211s and later A340-311s. Sabena A340-311 OO-SCZ is flying in formation with A330 OO-SFN. *Airbus Industrie*

Above: Air Mauritius had ordered six A340-300s to link the island with the important tourist industry. The first A340-312, 3B-NAT, was delivered on 18 May 1994. *Airbus Industrie*

Above: In November 1994, Air Canada ordered six A340-300s mainly on lease from ILFC. The order book eventually increased to 17, with further orders for the new long-range versions. The first aircraft for the airline was A340-313 CF-TNQ which was delivered on 15 June 1995. *Airbus Industrie*

Above: Known as the 'Celestar' by SIA, the A340-300Es started delivery in April 1996. The first A340-313, 9V-SJA, is shown on push-back at Perth Airport in January 1999 with the dark smoke of a bush fire in the background. *Author*

5. SALES AND SERVICE

Above: Lufthansa later also placed orders for up to 14 A340-300s and D-AIGF is seen at the moment of touchdown at Toulouse with the thrust reversers deployed. It was delivered to Lufthansa on 16 May 1994. *Airbus Industrie*

With the approval of the Airbus Industrie partners, the A340 was launched on 5 June 1987 in parallel with the twin-engined A330. At this time total commitments were for 130 aircraft, of which 89 were A340s, and the launch airlines included Lufthansa and Air France, who had consistently supported the Airbus products. By April 1989, 56 of the commitments had become firm orders. By the end of 1990, total orders for the A340 had reached 89 aircraft from 11 customers, with eight unidentified sales. Amongst these orders were 15 A340-211s for Lufthansa, seven A340-311s for Air France and eight for Iberia (another consistent supporter of Airbuses). The largest order had come from the Boeing-dominated market in the USA with 20 for Northwest Airlines together with 16 A330s, and Continental had placed orders for seven A340s and 13 A330s. Smaller fleets of A340s had been ordered by Sabena who wanted five A340-211s, UTA with six aircraft, Turk Hava Yollari (THY) with five, and two for TAP Air Portugal. An additional four A340s had been ordered by GPA and two by International Lease Finance Corporation (ILFC) for lease to operators.

After an overall successful year for the sale of all Airbus types in 1990, when with 404 orders the market share was increased to 35%, Airbus in common with the other airliner manufacturers expected a much poorer year in 1991 due to the Gulf crisis, which led to increased fuel prices and a reluctance on the part of passengers to travel, both on business and for holidays. Financial problems with the airlines also threatened some of the existing orders. However, on 28 March All Nippon Airways (ANA) signed for five A340s and options on a further five, with deliveries planned to commence in 1996. At the end of May, Northwest added a further four aircraft to its order. In June ILFC changed one of its A340 orders to an A330 and Air Lanka became a new customer at the beginning of August for five A340s, due to start deliveries in the spring of 1994. Also in August, TAP Air Portugal added two aircraft for delivery from early 1995.

In early August Singapore Airlines (SIA) announced that plans had been abandoned to buy up to 20 McDonnell Douglas (MDC) MD-11s valued at over $3 billion. The order had been conditional on the MD-11 being able to operate economically on the airline's long-haul sectors, particularly the 11,500km Singapore to Paris nonstop with defined payload capabilities. Although both MDC and engine suppliers Pratt & Whitney with the PW4000 had

Above: Although Sabena placed an early order for two A340-211s and three A340-311s, the aircraft were initially delivered to Air France under lease, who had taken a major interest in the Belgian airline. However, when the Air France share was transferred to Swissair, the aircraft were returned to the airline. Sabena A340-211 OO-SCW was originally delivered to Air France as F-GNIB on 9 June 1993 and joined Sabena on 26 June 1996. *Sabena*

offered last-minute improvements to overcome the problems with range, SIA switched to the CFM56-5C4-powered A340-300s with firm orders for seven aircraft, seven orders subject to reconfirmation and six options. The SIA order was worth $3.35 billion and deliveries were scheduled between 1995 and 1998.

By September new orders had been announced for Kuwait Airways with four aircraft, and an order for two A340s for Austrian Airlines was confirmed at the end of the month. In September and December contracts were placed for nine aircraft for unidentified airlines, bringing the total A340 orders to 127 aircraft, of which 24 had not been divulged.

At the end of February 1992, the first A340 took time off from the flight-development programme to make the first public appearance at the Asian Aerospace Show. With two firm customers in the region and memoranda of understanding from two others, including SIA, it was seen as a useful marketing exercise, and the flight to Singapore was used as a nonstop endurance exercise, contributing to the overall flight testing. The aircraft left Toulouse with a take-off weight of 248,000kg — 9,000kg below the maximum. The flight test equipment accounted for 22,000kg and 80,000kg of fuel was burned during the flight. On the return, a demonstration was made to Air Mauritius, which was a potential customer for a longer-range larger

aircraft than the Boeing 767-200ERs with the airline at the time. In March UTA, which had become part of Air France, added one A340 and in July Egyptair signed a letter of intent for three A340s with delivery by October 1994.

In September Gulf Air became the second Middle East airline to place a firm order for A340s, covering six firm and six options worth $500 million with deliveries planned to start in early 1994. In the same month, Philippine Airlines (PAL) placed firm orders for six A340-200s, with options on another four, to provide nonstop services to European destinations. With deliveries planned for 1994 and 1995, the airline would be the first carrier to operate the A340s in the Asia-Pacific region. At the end of September, GPA put in some doubt the four A340s on order, as did many other airlines, due to the economic difficulties with the markets. In October it was announced that Sabena would not take delivery of the five A340s it ordered as a launch customer, but instead they would be delivered to Air France who had bought a 25% share in the Belgian airline. Also in October, it was announced that China Eastern Airlines had placed the first order for the A330/A340 family in China, for five aircraft. China Aviation Supplies, the central purchasing organisation for China's airlines, had originally signed a memorandum of understanding for five A340s in 1991. The A340s were intended to open up new

Above: China Southwest Airlines took delivery of the first of two A340-313s, B-2389, on 9 November 1998. *Airbus Industrie*

Above: Emirates has placed orders for six A340-500s with options on six more. *Airbus Industrie*

Above: Air Lanka placed an order for five A340s, which was later reduced to three due to economic difficulties. The first A340-311, 4R-ADA, was delivered to the airline on 19 September 1994. *Airbus Industrie*

services from Shanghai to Europe, with the possibility of also using them on transpacific routes to the USA. At the end of November it was revealed that ILFC was in negotiation with Airbus and Boeing for combined orders for up to 90 aircraft. The A340 gained a further two aircraft as its share in the overall orders, bringing the total commitment to three aircraft.

SIA confirmed its order for seven A340s on 21 December 1992, bringing total orders for the type during the year to 22 aircraft, and overall orders to 121 with the Air France and Lufthansa aircraft participating in the route-proving programme. However, at the end of December Northwest announced major airliner cancellations, including both the A320 and A340, due to financial difficulties. Efforts were made by Airbus to renegotiate the contract to save some of the orders, as the second 50 of the 100 A320s had been cancelled as well as all 24 A340s. Although no Boeing orders were cancelled, a number of 757s and 747-400s were deferred. As a result of a number of cancellations, together with lower sales, the orders for jet airliners throughout the world dropped by 8% in 1992 over the previous year. The Airbus share of net orders fell from 23% to 13.3%.

The first A340 delivery was to Lufthansa on 2 February 1993 and was an A340-211, D-AIBA, the eighth aircraft off the production line. This aircraft was handed over at Frankfurt as the first of a firm order for 14 aircraft, with options on a further 15. Lufthansa expected to receive a further 10 A340s by

the end of the year, with the remainder in 1994. To take advantage of better weather conditions, the initial flight training started in Sharjah towards the end of February, with 37 pilots and check captains achieving A340 ratings ready for services to begin on 15 March. On service entry, the A340s replaced DC-10s on the Frankfurt to New York route, and as further aircraft were delivered they took over the services to Boston, Atlanta, Washington DC, Dallas and Houston. A second daily flight to New York was begun in August, with daily flights to Boston and Atlanta beginning in September, followed by Washington DC and São Paulo in October.

The A340s were introduced on routes which were the most competitive, replacing DC-10-30s and 747-200s which were phased out and sold. In some cases they also replaced the A310-300 on the North Atlantic routes, as the smaller aircraft was not built for such ranges and, although capable, suffered payload restrictions. The A340-300's capability of flying to the US West Coast made it ideal for flights to North America. The longer-range A340-200s were more suitable for South American and African services, where the routes are longer and the passenger demand lower.

At the end of February 1993, Virgin Atlantic Airways signed a letter of intent for the lease of four of the cancelled A340s, with three due for delivery by the end of the year and the fourth in 1994. The lease was signed in early April for the A340-300s, which were to pioneer routes for the higher-capacity Boeing 747-400s also being acquired by the airline.

Above: Singapore Airlines, which has a reputation for operating one of the world's youngest fleet of airliners, abandoned its plans to order MD-11s in August 1991 and ordered 14 A340-311s with six options, and later 10 of the A340-311E with 20 options. The first aircraft, 9V-SJA, was delivered to the airline on 17 April 1996 *Airbus Industrie*

The new aircraft replaced the earlier 747-100/200s which were due to have their leases expire by the end of the year. The first two A340s, delivered in October and November, were expected to replace 747s on the London to Tokyo service, the A340 being an excellent aircraft to develop routes, especially to destinations which stretch the 747's payload/range. The third aircraft delivered in December was for the London Gatwick to Boston services, raising the frequency to daily flights from the existing five a week with 747s. The final A340, scheduled for delivery by the end of 1994, was intended to substitute for a 747 on the daily service between London Heathrow and Boston, with later use on the London to San Francisco route planned for a start in May 1994. As the economic recovery progressed, Boeing 747-400s could be used on some of these routes, allowing the A340s to develop

Above: In September 1991 Kuwait Airways placed an order for four A340-311s, the first, 9K-ANA, being delivered to the airline on 29 March 1995. *Airbus Industrie*

Above: At the end of September 1991 Austrian Airlines ordered two A340-211s. The first, OE-LAG, is just seen at lift-off, being delivered on 28 February 1995.
Airbus Industrie

new destinations, possibly in Africa, Australia and some Japanese cities.

While in a bankruptcy situation in March 1993, Continental elected to cancel its firm orders for 20 A330/A340s, together with the options on a further 18 aircraft, the total value being some $4.2 billion. The contract, which had been signed in November 1989, included seven A340s, although Airbus had hoped to be able to negotiate a new contract covering various types and numbers of aircraft.

The first A340-300 was handed over to Air France on 26 February 1993 and was the 1,000th Airbus type to be delivered, the first A300B4 having been also delivered to Air France in May 1974. By the end of the year, Air France had taken delivery of nine out of a total of 19 A340s, seven having been ordered direct, with a further seven being the UTA order, and five on lease from Sabena. The first two A340s were introduced on the Paris to Washington DC service at the end of March, replacing 747s four times a week, and became a daily operation as more aircraft were delivered. A twice-weekly Paris to Mexico service followed, together with a Paris-Houston-Mexico City flight five-times-a-week. During August, Paris was linked with Buenos Aires and Santiago, and Recife-São Paulo. Towards the end of the year Montreal and Miami were added to the destinations.

In September 1993, a newly delivered Lufthansa A340 began operations with sensors designed to measure ozone and water vapour concentrations in the upper atmosphere, to determine the effects created by jet airliners. By April 1994, five A340s were allocated to the programme, operating with Lufthansa, Air France and Sabena, to collect data during the normal airline operations. The sampling equipment uses an inlet pipe outside the boundary layer mounted on the left side of the aircraft aft of the cockpit, and a pump, both coated in Teflon which has been found to preserve ozone. The air was collected in an ozone analyser and the water vapour content was measured using a humidity sensor.

Following a trouble-free service introduction, the technical reliability during the first year of operation achieved only 95.6% dispatch reliability, and at one stage fell to 94%. The delays were caused by three major problems, the principal one being the FAA ruling just before service entry that the single inner fuel tank should be split into two compartments. The extensive changes included fitting new fuel probes, wiring and computers which did not have sufficient time to achieve full reliability before service entry but had improved after the first year. There were some problems with the vacuum-type toilets, which had to be modified. Also there were problems with ducting and temperature control in the air-conditioning

Above: In July 1992 Egyptair ordered three A340-200s, the first, SU-GBM, being delivered on 26 November 1996. This aircraft is seen after entry into service. *Egyptair*

system, which were also cured. The combined improvements brought dispatch reliability to almost 98% by mid-1994.

The depressed world economic conditions and reduced airliner orders continued to cause concern, and there were reports in July 1993 that TAP Air Portugal was having to consider cancelling the order for four A340s, due for delivery in early 1994. The World Bank had reservations about the Sri Lankan economy and the ability of the country to support the acquisition of five A340s costing $700 million, an amount close to the total annual economic aid received by Sri Lanka, which would make the servicing of the debt difficult. Due to pressure from the World Bank, Air Lanka was having to consider cancelling its order for five A340s, and renegotiate a lease for a smaller fleet.

Philippine Airlines was considering the deferment of some of its A340 deliveries because of a clash with the delivery of the first Boeing 747-400, which had overstretched the training resources of air and ground crews. The first A340 was already in production and due for delivery in April 1994, while the 747-400 had arrived the previous November. In December, negotiations were continuing with Airbus, PAL and Cathay Pacific Airways, resulting in the PAL A340s being taken by Cathay on two-year operating leases, the first aircraft arriving in October 1994, with all in service by mid-1995. This paved the way for an order from Cathay for six higher-gross-weight A340-300Xs launched by SIA, and options on a further six, with deliveries starting in mid-1996. Cathay required the A340s for selected long thin European routes from Hong Kong to Amsterdam, Manchester, Rome and Zurich, with the aircraft later being available to develop new services. After months of protracted negotiations, PAL reached agreement with Airbus Industrie, cancelling the order for six A340-200s and replacing it with a six-year lease for four aircraft starting in 1996. Cathay still took the four aircraft on lease as planned, passing them on to PAL as the new higher-gross-weight A340s became available. The first of the interim-leased A340-200s was delivered to Cathay in November 1994.

By October 1993 confirmed orders for the A340 were 112 aircraft with

Above: Gulf Air A340-312 A40-LB was delivered to the airline on 18 July 1994 and was leased for a while to Air Mauritius. *Airbus Industrie*

Above: In October 1992 China Eastern ordered five A340-300s, with the first A340-313 delivered on 15 May 1996. B-2382 is seen on the flight line at Toulouse ready for delivery on 25 July. *Airbus Industrie*

13 delivered. The A340-200s were in operation with Lufthansa, Qatar Amiri Flight, the Brunei government and Sabena, while the A340-300s were in service with Air France and THY. New recent sales included three A340-300s for Air Mauritius. Virgin Atlantic took delivery of the first of four A340s on 21 November 1993, commencing London Heathrow to Boston services on 8 December. In April 1994 Virgin began operations with the A340s between London and Hong Kong.

In June 1994, Singapore Airlines appeared ready to place a massive $3.5 billion order for new airliners, effectively doubling the fleet size by 2003 and maintaining its stature as the operator of the

Above: Frankfurt is the home base for the Lufthansa fleet and a major international hub. An A340 is seen on turnaround with other members of the Airbus family in the background. *Lufthansa/Werner Krüger*

Above: Lufthansa A340-311 D-AIGH on push-back at Frankfurt on 1 April 1998.
Author

youngest fleet of any major airline. In addition to the seven A340s already on order with 13 options, a further 10 A340s were being considered, along with Boeing 747-400s and 777s. It was not uncommon for SIA to place major orders while the market was depressed, as it resulted in bargain prices on aircraft being delivered into the next century.

The economy of the southern Indian Ocean island of Mauritius is based on the export of textiles and sugar, with tourism the third-highest earner. However, to maintain the fragile balance of the island's ecology, it was essential to stay with the high-yield luxury end of the tourist market, bringing fewer but higher-paying visitors. Air Mauritius is the mainstay of the tourism industry, 80% of its

Above: For the long-haul flights on the A340s, Lufthansa has provided a more comfortable seat for the business class passengers with a 125° incline and more space. *Lufthansa/Ingo Wagner*

passengers being tourists, making the airline an instrument of the economic development of the country. The first A340-300, seating up to 295 passengers, was delivered to the airline on 19 May 1994, replacing the first of three 747SPs leased from SAA. Four more A340s were delivered up to April 1998, replacing the other two 747SPs and expanding the fleet capacity. Three of the A340s were bought direct from Airbus, while the other two were leased from ILFC for an initial period of four years. The airline then had the option of extending the lease for a further three years or buying the aircraft outright. The arrival of the initial A340 in Mauritius increased available seat-kilometres for the current year to four billion, which was a 7% increase over the financial year of 1993-4. This increased the seats available by 5% to 865,000 and cargo capacity by 31% to 16,500 tonnes annually. The airline planners anticipate an overall passenger load of 950,000 by 2002. The A340 had much lower fuel consumption and half the maintenance costs of the Boeing 747SP and in the selection process, the A340-300 was chosen on the basis of lower costs, compared with the closest competitors; availability; passenger capacity; range, and the four-engine configuration which avoided the Erops restrictions. Although Air Mauritius held options for four more aircraft for delivery up to 2006, the limited capacity of the tourist industry made conversion of these options unlikely. The airline signed a commercial co-operation agreement with Lufthansa to provide total technical support, and pilot training and line service tuition for four training captains, who then took

Above: **For the long-haul flights, Lufthansa has also improved the comfort levels in the economy class cabin, giving additional space.**
Lufthansa/Ingo Wagner

responsibility for their own cockpit crews. All simulator training was at Lufthansa's Frankfurt base.

Following the earlier economic difficulties the Sri Lankan government finally sanctioned the purchase of three A340-300s for Air Lanka in September 1994. The timing was critical as the first aircraft was due for delivery the same month, the second in October, and the third in February 1995. A management group within the airline was tasked with deciding the best way to utilise the aircraft, and how the financial burden would be spread across the airline and the government, which was the guarantor. All options were considered: from operating the aircraft with the airline, to leasing or sale to other airlines.

While operating the Tokyo to London Heathrow service on 19 September 1994, a Virgin Atlantic A340 crew suffered fuel misreading and two flight management guidance envelope computer (FMGEC) software problems. One of the software problems resulted in the loss of both pilots' map displays, and the other could have caused an autopilot turn in the wrong direction from a heading of 180°. The aircraft was landed safely from a hand-flown surveillance radar approach after the crew had declared a full emergency. On shutdown it was found that 4.5 tonnes of fuel remained.

In its report on the incident, the UK Air Accidents Investigation Branch (AAIB) noted that new airliners are bound to suffer from minor teething troubles after service entry. Some faults will be found before entry into service, but still allow certification, while others will have to be corrected before certification. The AAIB were therefore concerned to know if the JAA was aware of some of the more significant difficulties of the A340 fuel and flight management system before certification was granted. By February 1995, Airbus had identified all the problems and

Above: In 1994 Cathay Pacific Airways ordered six higher-gross-weight A340-300s, taking on lease in the interim the PAL A340-200s, the order being cancelled for six aircraft and being replaced by a lease for four aircraft. Cathay A340-313 VR-HXB was delivered on 20 June 1996 and is now registered B-HXB. *Airbus Industrie*

Above: Originally delivered to Air France as F-GNIC on 25 June 1993, this A340-211 returned to Sabena in March 1996 and was re-registered OO-SCX soon afterwards. *Airbus Industrie*

modifications were in hand for the world fleet. The fuel problem had been tackled by adding five additional sensors in each inner tank and making a software upgrade. The map display fault had been a problem with the A320, and although the incidence had been reduced, the basic fault still needed to be

Above: By October 1993 A340-311s were in service with THY, TC-JDN being delivered on 19 August 1997 as the fifth out of an order for six aircraft. The A340s operate the airline's long-haul services from Istanbul to New York, Chicago and Miami in the USA, Bangkok/Singapore, Beijing, Tokyo and Osaka in Asia, and Johannesburg/Cape Town in South Africa. TC-JDN is seen on approach to Heathrow on 1 April 1999. *Nick Granger*

Above: Virgin Atlantic took delivery of its first A340-311, G-VBUS, on 26 November 1993. Its second delivery was G-VSKY on 21 January 1994, seen at Heathrow on 1 May 1999 preparing for departure. *Author*

solved. The autopilot turn had already been cured on most aircraft at the time of the incident, and was soon sorted out on the remainder.

By November 1994 34 aircraft had been delivered and new orders included six A340-300s for China Southern and six A340-300s for Air Canada. At the beginning of 1995, SIA signed a contract for 10 of what had become the A340-300E long-haul version, with options on a further 20 aircraft. The CFM56-5C4-powered aircraft had the maximum take-off weight increased to 271,220kg and its

range extended to 13,230km (7,150nm).

Towards the end of January 1995, ANA reached an agreement with Airbus Industrie to order 10 A321s, but to defer the delivery of the five A340-300s until at least 2000 from the planned start of deliveries from late 1996. In early 1995 it was reported that Region Air of Singapore had ordered an A340 and was considering the purchase of a second aircraft, both being for lease to Vietnam Airlines. The airline had a requirement for up to five long-range wide-bodied airliners from 1996 onwards, but was

Above: The first A340-312, A40-LA, was delivered to Gulf Air on 17 May 1994. A340-312 A40-LE was initially delivered on lease to Egyptair on 13 October 1995, joining Gulf Air on 27 June 1997. It is seen in a hybrid colour scheme on approach to Heathrow in September 1997. *Nick Granger*

Above: 3B-NAV was the third A340-313 delivered to Air Mauritius on 31 March 1995 to replace Boeing 747SPs on long-haul services. This aircraft is seen on approach to Heathrow in August 1995. *Nick Granger*

short of funding. The first of four A340-300s was delivered to Kuwait Airways on 29 March 1995, powered by the 150kN (34,000lb) thrust CFM56-5C4 engines, the most powerful of the type. The A340s were introduced on the services to New York via London and Frankfurt, and on direct flights to Mumbai (Bombay), Bangkok and Manila.

With orders already confirmed for 10 A340-300Es, and options on 20 more, SIA announced a competition between Airbus and Boeing, as well as General Electric, Pratt & Whitney and Rolls-Royce, for the replacement of some of the short and medium-haul A310s used on Asian services. Airbus

had the A330 and A340 on offer, in competition with the early version of the Boeing 777.

Air France was suffering from financial difficulties in 1995, having threatened to cancel all outstanding new airliner orders in January. By the middle of the year, the airline had reached an agreement with Airbus, allowing two already completed long-range A340s to be delivered within four months, but it would be allowed to return two A340-200s by the end of 1998. Negotiations continued on the ultimate fate of five other long-range A340s due for delivery by 1997, with the possibility of cancellation or deferment of the delivery.

Above: Despite economic difficulties, Air Lanka took delivery of the first of three A340-300s, 4R-ADA, on 19 September 1994. The second aircraft, 4R-ADB, was delivered on 6 October and is seen on approach to Heathrow on 1 April 1999. *Nick Granger*

Above: TAP Air Portugal took delivery of its first A340-312, CS-TOA, on 22 December 1994. This aircraft is seen on approach to London Heathrow on 1 April 1999. *Nick Granger*

The first A340 deliveries to North America were in June 1995, when the first two -300s were received by Air Canada, entering service on 30 June from Toronto to Vancouver and Seoul with a two-class cabin layout. Two more aircraft were delivered in 1996, and the remaining four in 1997. In July, Air Canada followed up with a commitment for two of the planned ultra-long-range A340-8000s as part of the existing order, but Airbus needed around 12 orders to launch the 14,825km (8,000nm) range

aircraft. The 232-seat aircraft was in direct competition with the shrunk long-range Boeing 777-100X, but Airbus was hopeful of a service entry in the first half of 1997, giving a two-year lead over the Boeing development. In the search for enough customers to justify the launch of the thin-capacity ultra-long-range airliner, the Asian region was expected to have a significant need, with both Cathay and SIA regarded as the strongest potential launch customers. Cathay had a requirement for a

Above: The first delivery of an A340 to Kuwait Airways was in March 1995, and all four A340-313s were delivered by July with services soon commencing. A340-313 9K-ANB is seen ready for departure from Heathrow in September 1998 en route between Kuwait and New York. *Nick Granger*

Above: The first North American delivery of A340s was to Air Canada in June 1995 when two aircraft were received and put into operation on services from Toronto to Asia. Air Canada A340-313 C-FYKX was delivered to the airline on 19 November 1996, and is seen ready for departure at the now closed Hong Kong Kai Tak airport in April 1998. *Author*

nonstop all-the-year-round service between Hong Kong and Toronto, like Air Canada, as well as the launch of new services to New York and Chicago. SIA had a need for an aircraft to operate ultra-long-range routes nonstop from Singapore to the US West Coast. The A340-8000 would, in fact, offer a capability of flying around the world with one stop.

Also in July 1995, Egyptair ordered three A340s with options on two more with deliveries due to start at the end of 1996. The airline planned to open up new routes from Cairo to Japan, Australia and the US West Coast. At the end of July 1995, the first high-gross-weight A340-300E of 17 for SIA was flown from Toulouse. Power came from the 150kN (34,000lb) thrust CFM56-5C4 engines, the maximum take-off weight being increased from 257 tonnes to 271 tonnes. The wings were reinforced to accommodate an extra 2,400 litres of fuel in the

Above: Like Lufthansa, Air Canada is a member of the Star Alliance and A340-313 C-FYLD has been painted in the members' colours, with Air Canada in the lead. This aircraft was delivered to the airline on 29 April 1997. *Air Canada*

Above: Air Canada operates the A340-300s in a two-class layout. The forward cabin is known as Executive First with two aisles and six-abreast seats. *Air Canada*

Above: The main cabin on the Air Canada A340-300s is known as Hospitality Class with eight-abreast seating and central overhead bins in addition to the ones at the sides. *Air Canada*

centre and outer tanks, bringing total capacity to 141,000 litres. Cruise efficiency was also improved by a twist in the outer wing section.

At the end of 1995 it was announced that three of the A340s previously ordered by China Aviation Supplies (CASC) would be delivered to Air China to replace four Boeing 747SPs on long-haul passenger services and government VIP flights. The six A340s ordered by CASC in November 1993 had been intended for China Southern but it selected the Boeing 777, and China Eastern was the most likely operator to take the remaining three A340s.

The new year of 1996 started well with an order for two high-capacity A340-300s from Austrian Airlines worth $320 million for delivery in 1997 and 1999. The new aircraft were to be configured with 297 seats in two classes and would supplement or replace the existing A340-200s on the services to Johannesburg, Beijing and Tokyo, as well as being used to inaugurate new services.

In 1995, Airbus introduced the concept of a passenger sleeping compartment installed in the front cargo hold of the long-range A340, the compartment consisting of five sets of bunk beds in

Above: At the end of 1995 it was announced that three A340-300s would be allocated to Air China. A340-313 B-2385 was the first of these and was delivered on 7 October 1997. *Airbus Industrie*

Above left: In early 1996 Austrian Airlines ordered a pair of A340-300s to expand the existing services with the A340-200s. Both versions are configured in a three-class layout, the first class being six abreast and known as Grand Class. *Austrian Airlines*

Above right: The Austrian Airlines Economy Class has eight-abreast seating in the A340s. *Austrian Airlines*

three separate cabins. The first airline to order this sleeper compartment was Virgin Atlantic in January 1996 in an A340 due for delivery in mid-1997 for use by the first class passengers on long-haul services, possibly including the planned new ones to Singapore and Sydney. The aircraft allocated to this order was the seventh for Virgin and had not been announced previously.

In March 1996 ILFC announced further orders with Airbus and Boeing including 12 of the higher maximum take-off weight of 270-tonne A340-300s with deliveries starting in May 1997 to undisclosed operators. In the same month, the Sultan of Brunei

selected an ultra-long-range A340-8000 as an addition to his growing VIP fleet of jet airliners. The new A340-8000 was expected to be the first of the variant off the Toulouse production line and was scheduled for delivery in 1997, but due to financial problems was not accepted. By fitting auxiliary fuel tanks, the special A340 has a range of more than 14,800km (8,000nm), enabling the Sultan to fly from Brunei to destinations in the USA and Europe. The Sultan's fleet already included two A340-200s, the entire fleet being flown on contract by Lufthansa.

On 31 March 1996, Sabena began operations with an A340-200, replacing a Boeing 747-200 on

Above: The first A340-313 for Iberia, EC-GGS, was delivered on 29 February 1996 and is seen at London Gatwick on 4 September 1997. *Nick Granger*

Above: The first A340 to be delivered to China was A340-313 B-2380 for China Eastern on 15 May 1996. The second aircraft, B-2381, followed on 29 May and is seen on final approach to Hong Kong Kai Tak in April 1998. *Author*

the Brussels to New York service. The Belgian airline dry-leased its fleet of five A340s to its then shareholder Air France, but with Swissair becoming the second major shareholder, four of the aircraft were progressively returned to Sabena, the remaining one having been destroyed by fire at Paris Charles de Gaulle Airport soon after delivery. In April, Air Mauritius inaugurated a direct weekly service from Mauritius to Manchester with A340s, increasing to twice-weekly by the end of the year. With thrice-weekly rights from its home base to Australia, the airline was promoting services from

the UK to Australia via Mauritius as an alternative to the more usual routes via Singapore.

On 25 April 1996, SIA took delivery of the first two of 17 A340-300Es, with four more delivered during the year. The new 276-seat A340s were used initially to serve the relatively short-range destinations to Bangkok and Jakarta, as well as Melbourne and later Sydney. On the Australian routes, the A340s replaced Boeing 747s, and increased frequencies to daily flights from five times a week. The A340s with SIA were initially approved for a maximum take-off weight of 271 tonnes, but

Above: The first A340-212, SU-GBN, was delivered to Egyptair on 20 December 1996. It is seen ready for departure from Heathrow on 27 May 1998. *Author*

Above: The first three A340-300s were delivered to Cathay Pacific in Hong Kong on 22 June 1996 to begin the replacement of the A340-200s for PAL. A340-313 B-HXH was delivered to Cathay on 31 March 1998 and is seen on 6 April moving towards the departure point at Hong Kong Kai Tak airport. *Author*

Left: PAL started receiving the A340-211s from Cathay in 1996. A340-211 F-OHPF was delivered to the airline on 27 September 1996. *PAL*

Above: The first A340-300 was delivered to PAL in June 1997, joining the A340-200s. A340-313 F-OHPK, which was delivered on 24 June 1997, is seen on final approach to Heathrow in April 1998. *Nick Granger.*

within a month of operation there was an increase to 275 tonnes achieved by a change in certification paperwork. The weight bonus allowed the carriage of an extra 3,000 litres of fuel, extending the range to 13,500km (7,300nm) and permitting a direct nonstop daily service to Paris which started in October.

BWIA had originally ordered two A340-300s from Airbus in 1995, which were scheduled for delivery in late 1996 to replace the rather old TriStar 500s used for services to Europe. However, the airline was suffering some financial difficulties, making the acquisition of much-needed new equipment difficult, and negotiations were restarted with Airbus in mid-1996 to find a solution. The order was finally cancelled in August, the alternative being to refurbish the TriStars for further service.

The first A340 to be delivered to China arrived with China Eastern Airlines on 15 May 1996 at the Shanghai base. Services with 289-seat three-class arrangement were inaugurated in June to Los Angeles, although later the aircraft were also used on the shorter route to Hong Kong. Virgin increased its A340 order book by ordering two more A340-300s in May 1996 for delivery a year later. The new aircraft were intended to further develop the network in Asia-Pacific, including Australasia, the USA and South Africa, with further possibilities in the Caribbean. The first A340-300 for Cathay Pacific arrived in Hong Kong on 22 June 1996 to begin the replacement of the four A340-200s leased from PAL. Cathay increased its order for the A340-300Es to nine aircraft

in September 1996, for delivery during the second half of 1998, to be used on selected Asian routes and also intended for services to destinations in Europe and North America.

In July Airbus received its first order from General Electric Capital Aviation Services (GECAS) for 45 aircraft with 45 options. While the bulk of the order was for the narrow-bodied A319/A320/A321 family, five A340-300s were included for delivery to unspecified airlines starting in 1999.

In September 1996, Swissair was evaluating a new long-range medium/high-capacity airliner to replace its five Boeing 747-300s from the year 2000. The projected A340-600 with around 375 seats in a three-class layout, with a range capability of more than 13,000km (7,000nm), was a contender. Airbus had held the second airliner advisory meeting at around the same time, which was helping to define the A340-500/600 specification with around 15 potential customers. At this time the biggest question mark was the lack of a defined engine, although General Electric was due to present its proposals the following month for the stretched and rewinged derivatives.

The fire on the ground in a Malaysia Airlines A330-300 in January 1997, which caused some $30 million worth of damage, was the latest of a number of major fires with A330/340s, including an Air Mauritius A340-300 suffering $28 million worth of damage in October 1996 and the total loss of an Air France A340 in January 1994. The Air France aircraft was so badly damaged that the cause of the fire was

Above: In November 1998 Aerolineas Argentinas announced its intention to introduce a fleet of A340-200 and -300s, the aircraft coming mainly from PAL who had become bankrupt. The first of the Argentinian A340-200s was ready for delivery in March 1999. *Airbus Industrie*

difficult to determine, but the Air Mauritius A340 fire was caused by an overheating electrically-driven hydraulic pump during routine ground maintenance. Three of these pumps are used as an in-flight back-up to engine-driven pumps working the three aircraft hydraulic systems. One is located in the starboard main wheel well and is also used on the ground to operate the cargo doors. As a precaution, Airbus advised that the pumps be deactivated, pending their replacement with alternatives.

In March 1997 SIA was still considering an order for at least 10 ultra-long-range aircraft to open new services and increase existing frequencies to the USA. The two options being evaluated were the A340-500 and the Boeing 777-200X, both of which needed a launch order. Flights of up to 18hr endurance were expected to be required, as the Boeing 747-400 used on the routes had to fly via Hong Kong, Tokyo and Taipei because of payload/range limitations. Because of the long-elapsed time of flight, comfort levels would have to be increased, with wider seat pitch, enlarged first and business class cabins and higher-cost economy seats. About half the 250-seat cabin would be occupied by first and business class passengers, and the seat-kilometre costs of the aircraft would have to be capable of generating a profit. In April, SIA also became the first operator to specify for the Airbus fleet the Future Air Navigation System-A (FANS-A) to be installed in the long-haul A340-300s. Certification of the new equipment was scheduled

for April 1998 following flight testing in the company's A340 development aircraft, using initially a dedicated ground station at Toulouse followed by active tests worldwide. The equipment was capable of retrofit to the aircraft in service as well as being installed in new production, and all FANS-A-capable aircraft are equipped with Smiths datalink control display units in the cockpit allowing text communications with air traffic controllers, as well as satellite communications equipment.

The first A340-300 for Philippine Airlines was delivered in June 1997, joining the four A340-200s already in service. This new A340-300 had a 264-seat three-class cabin layout and was part of a fleet renewal programme involving A320s, A330s and A340s over a period of 20 months.

In August 1997 Airbus made the first step towards a programme launch of the A340-500/600, with commitments from Air Canada and Virgin Atlantic. Air Canada signed a letter of intent for five A330s and three long-range higher-gross-weight A340s in phase 1 of a three-phase programme to replace Boeing 747-100/200 Classics. Phase 2, due to be confirmed in March 1998, was five new Rolls-Royce Trent-powered A340 growth models consisting of two 308-seat A340-500s and three 360-seat A340-600s, with options on a further 10 aircraft. The new A340-500/600s were required for additional services from Toronto to the new Hong Kong airport, where additional capacity was expected to be available. Phase 3 covered options

Above: On 10 November 1998 Air Tahiti Nui took delivery of A340-211 F-OITN which had previously served with Air France as F-GLZD. *Airbus Industrie*

on a mix of a further eight A330/340s as required, to replace three 747-400 Combies from 2000. The second and third phases were dependent upon Canadian government approval. Virgin was interested in up to eight A340-600s with options on eight more, with deliveries starting in 2002. The new larger aircraft were intended for increasing traffic on services to the US West Coast and Asia. In addition, Virgin ordered two additional A340-300s, bringing the total fleet to 10 aircraft. The contract was signed by Virgin Chairman, Richard Branson, for eight Rolls-Royce Trent-powered A340-600s in December 1997, with options on eight more, deliveries to start in 2002.

Also in August, Olympic decided to order two A340-300s with options on two more, with deliveries starting in 1998, to replace the 747-200 Classic fleet. At the end of the same month Cathay announced plans to order up to 20 new wide-body airliners, including seven more A340-300s with six A330-300s, and optional substitution rights to switch to the new A340-500 ultra-long-haul aircraft. The planned large-scale growth of the airline would allow it to take advantage of the increased slots available after Kai Tak was replaced by the new Chep Lap Kok airport. The new additions to the fleet also allowed for increased frequency of existing services.

Air China took delivery of the first of three A340-300s on 8 October 1997, followed by the second later in the same month and the third in November. Services commenced by the end of October, initially on domestic routes from Beijing to Guangzhou, Hainan, Shanghai and Ürümqi.

International scheduled flights commenced in December to Fukuoka in Japan, and Paris. Consideration was being given to ordering a fourth A340 to allow one to be used for government VIP flights, replacing a Boeing 747SP. Also in October, Qantas announced that an evaluation was taking place for a 300-seat airliner, with the A340 and Boeing 777 as contenders.

There was an incident at London Heathrow on 5 November when Virgin A340-300, G-VSKY, with 114 passengers and crew on board made a landing with the port main landing gear locked up. No one was hurt, but one runway was blocked for nearly 24hr while the aircraft was removed for repairs. The cause was found to be a loose brake-rod which fouled the mechanism in the undercarriage bay.

In November, the launch of the A340-500/600 developments came a step closer with a letter of intent for up to 12 aircraft from Taiwan's EVA Air, six being firm requirements, with six options. Other potential customers were Egyptair, Emirates, Lufthansa, SIA and Swissair, and in November Swissair selected up to five A340-600s with options as a replacement for five 747-300s and two with the Belgian partner, Sabena. At the same time Lufthansa was close to finalising an order for an unspecified number of the new A340s, the decision being expected to be made in early December. The Lufthansa A340-500/600s were to replace up to eight of the 747-200s, and also to provide an expansion of the long-haul fleet. Emirates signed a letter of intent for six A340-500s with options on six, bringing total commitments to 78 aircraft from seven airlines and allowing the formal launch of the new programme. Emirates required an aircraft capable of operating direct flights from Dubai to New York, Sydney and ultimately Los Angeles, the main competition coming from the proposed Boeing 777-200X ultra-long-range development. The Emirates contract was confirmed in September 1998, the options having increased to 10, and deliveries starting in 2002.

In January 1998, Egyptair signed a firm contract with Airbus for four 400-seat A340-600s, covering two orders and two options for delivery from 2003. Meanwhile, SIA had asked for fresh proposals from Airbus and Boeing for the A340-500 and the Boeing 777-200X for the demanding Singapore to Los Angeles route where break-even load factors were critical, needing to be in the region of 85% to 90%. SIA required a still air range of 16,260km (8,790nm), with additional fuel for diversion, holding and go-around, giving a year-round load of 200 passengers to the US West Coast. Depending upon the number of routes to be operated by SIA, the number of aircraft required was between six and 10. By May the A340-500 was considered the favourite for the SIA order, with the decision made in the middle of the month for five aircraft, plus five options for delivery from 2002, while options on the current A340s remained.

In April, Lufthansa confirmed its earlier commitment for 10 A340-600s with deliveries starting in 2003. Air Canada also added a further A340-300 on a seven-year lease from ILFC for delivery in 1999. In August 1998, it was reported that ILFC was about to place a $1.5 billion order for five A340-500/600s and five options, the first two aircraft being -600s, and the remainder -500s, with deliveries to start in 2002. This took orders, options and commitments for the new versions to 110 aircraft.

Sabena A340 OO-SCW was severely damaged at Brussels Airport on 29 August 1998 when the starboard main landing gear failed at the end of the landing run inbound from New York. Following the failure, the centre gear also collapsed, the right wing and engines hitting the ground, and the aircraft rotated through about 100° before coming to a halt. The 255 passengers and 10 crew evacuated the aircraft and it was found that the two-wheel rear section of the starboard bogie had separated, and the main gear barrel was broken near the retraction actuator. The damage was expected to take about four months to repair.

With the worsening economic situation in Asia during 1998, Philippine Airlines went into receivership in June and announced drastic cutbacks in services. The airline was reduced to 14 aircraft operating 21 routes with 200 aircrew. A major part of the leased fleet was grounded and the airline was planning to dispose of up to eight A340s. The economic situation also brought a loss to EVA Air resulting in the airline abandoning plans to acquire up to 12 of the new A340s to avoid over-capacity.

On a more positive note, Iberia announced plans in September 1998 to add further A340-300s to its fleet. The memorandum of understanding covered six firm commitments for delivery to start in November 1999, and five options, and was in addition to eight firm and four options placed in October 1989. Iberia currently operates the A340s from Madrid to destinations in Latin America, South Africa and the USA, and the expansion was expected to allow greater frequency to Latin America. The following month, Virgin increased the order for A340-600s by two aircraft to a total of 10, the newly ordered aircraft to be delivered by 2004. By the end of 1998 orders for the new ultra-long-range developments had reached around 120 for nine airlines, worth about $15 billion.

In November Aerolineas Argentinas announced the intention to start the introduction of a fleet of 12 A340s from March 1999, the fleet including four 225-seat A340-200s and two 264-seat A340-300s. The MOU included six further 309-seat A340-600s for delivery from 2004, the aircraft being required for use on services to Europe and New Zealand.

Early in the New Year of 1999, SAS announced the selection of the A330/340 family for the planned long-haul fleet renewal, but was waiting for cost-cutting targets to be met before confirming the order. The planned fleet was expected to include six A340s with five options on either type, and deliveries were planned to start in 2000 although the decision was not expected until the end of the year.

The A340 with its future developments has therefore become firmly established in competition with the Boeing 777 in a number of markets, and will be particularly valuable in replacing earlier versions of the Boeing 747 as well as developing new long-range routes later capable of taking higher-capacity airliners.

6. FUTURE DEVELOPMENTS

Above: By October 1997 Air Canada had signed a letter of intent for five of the high-capacity A340-600s for its ultra-long-haul routes, particularly for Toronto to Hong Kong all the year round. *Airbus Industrie*

Some of the development of the A340 has naturally been mentioned in the chapter covering the sales and service, but it is necessary to cover the full potential of this advanced airliner. Even as early as the end of 1992, Airbus was offering a version of the aircraft optimised for short and medium-haul routes as a possible alternative to the big-twins. Referred to as the A340 light, the aircraft could be certificated to a lower maximum take-off weight (MTOW) of around 235 tonnes instead of the existing 257 tonnes, with direct operating costs reduced by around 1%. On offer to existing operators, savings would come from derating the engines, and from reduced landing fees and navigation service charges. The A340 light impinged on the market potential of the A330 and other twin-engined airliners, the four-engined aircraft with its lower installed thrust being capable of fulfilling some market needs without the restrictions of satisfying the Erops requirements, and making the A340 economical

for the shorter sectors as well as long-range operations. Major structural changes would not be required as the savings could be achieved by certificating at a lower MTOW.

As a contrast, Airbus was also studying growth versions of the A340-300 in late 1992, in particular for the SIA requirement on the critical nonstop Singapore to Paris route with a great circle distance of 12,350km. The confirmation of this version was delayed by six months to allow the incorporation of the structural modifications to cope with the higher all-up weight. One of the major changes was the redesign of the Dowty Aerospace-designed main landing gear to support the 271-tonne MTOW of the developed version. Other changes included strengthening the main wing-box, new landing gear attachments and reinforcement of pick-up structure of the main and nose gear. The increased MTOW led to a reduction in the centre of gravity range of the A340, and aerodynamic changes included a wing twist, changing the angle of incidence at the wingtip, and realignment of the engine thrust vector.

By early 1995, Airbus was in discussions with some operators about a proposed A340-8000, which was in effect a high-gross-weight A340-300 with an 8,000nm (14,825km) range, achieved by combining the stronger wing of the -300 with an auxiliary fuel tank already specified by some airlines. The MTOW would be increased from 271 tonnes to 275 tonnes, and lower-deck passenger beds and toilets could be launched with this version. Further thoughts included additional passenger seats below the main deck forward of the wing, which would be the first time a wide-bodied airliner would be certificated with passengers seated on the lower deck during take-off and landing. By re-engining with 178kN (40,000lb) thrust engines, the aircraft would have a one-stop round-the-world capability.

Towards the end of 1995 Airbus confirmed the development of the ultra-long-range A340-8000 with the wings strengthened to allow three extra fuel tanks to be fitted in the forward part of the rear hold, to give a range of 15,000km with 230 seats in a three-class configuration. Only one example was built. In the first quarter of 1996, Airbus announced a super-stretch version of the A340, designated the A340-600, as direct competition for the Boeing 777-300. With a range of 12,400km, the -600 would be able to carry up to 370 passengers in three classes, and, depending upon engine availability, could be launched by 1997 with service entry from 2001. Commonality with existing versions was a requirement, the basic wing having modest increases in span and chord, with some of the extra required lift coming from proposed foreplanes on the forward fuselage to help reduce drag by off-loading the tail. The fuselage was to

Above: Launched as a combined programme in December 1997, design of the A340-500/600 is progressing well. By January 1998 wind tunnel tests of the A340-500 had commenced in the DNW wind tunnel in the Netherlands using a 1:11-scale model. *Daimler-Benz Aerospace*

Above: The super-stretch A340-600 was launched by Airbus in early 1996 as a direct competitor to the Boeing 777-300ER. *Airbus Industrie*

be increased in capacity by inserting plugs forward and behind the centre-section.

By mid-1996 the range requirement had increased to 15,700km (8,500nm) by combining the fuselage of the A340-300 with the proposed wing changes and new engines of the -600, as an alternative to the smaller 14,825km-range A340-8000. The airlines wanted the 225kN (51,000lb) thrust engines proposed for the -600 to be fitted to the A340-300, resulting in an A340-500. The rejection of the A340-8000 was as a result of Air Canada deciding to drop a commitment for two A340-8000s because with the fuselage reduced in length by 4.26m from the -300, it was not big enough to be economical on routes such as Toronto to Hong Kong all the year round. The A340-500 would have room for around 310 passengers, which because of the extra two fuselage frames to accommodate the -600 larger wing, would be slightly more than the -300. The launch timetable was still planned for around early 1997 with service entry from 2000/2001. The development costs for the A340-600 were estimated to be at least $1 billion for the airframe alone, with the powerplant costs paid for by the engine supplier. A further option being studied was a stretched 11,300km version of the A340-300, referred to as the A340-400.

As already detailed in the powerplants chapter, Airbus signed an exclusive six-month study contract with General Electric in April 1996 for the development of the engine to meet the A340-600 227kN (51,000lb) thrust requirement, which had increased to 249kN by September. To maintain as much commonality as possible, the A340-600 wing used the existing front and rear spars of the A340-200/300 wing, but had the area increased by 56sq m (600sq ft) to 420sq m. To achieve this the span was increased by 3.5m to 63.8m with the existing winglets retained, and the chord increased from the root, accommodated by a three-frame plug inserted in the fuselage centre-section. The wing fuel tank capacity was expected to increase by about 25%. The overall fuselage stretch was planned to be 20 to 22 frames, increasing the length to some 75m. With the take-off weight increased to 330,000kg, the twin-wheeled centre main landing gear would need replacing with a pair of side-by-side twin-wheeled units to retain existing pavement levels. The A340-600 had grown to an aircraft capable of carrying up to 375 passengers over distances of 12,950km (7,000nm). The simple stretch A340-400 was still being considered with a 12-frame cabin extension to accommodate 340 passengers in a three-class layout over ranges of 11,290km, while retaining the existing wing and powerplants. The A340-400 could be available for service entry in 1999 if there was sufficient demand. However, by the end of September Airbus had dropped plans to develop the A340-400, deciding instead to concentrate resources on the A340-500/600 programme.

Following close consultation from May 1996 with the growing customer base in focus groups, including Lufthansa, Air France, Virgin, Swissair,

Iberia and Alitalia, by early October Airbus had made the decision to develop the A340-500/600 derivatives, even though there were doubts with the engine and no airline had signed up at that stage. The -500 ultra-long-haul version was in effect a higher-gross-weight version of the -300, and the stretched -600 had the cabin capacity increased by around 25%. Both aircraft used the same enlarged wing with a 63.6m span, with a tapered spanwise wing-box inserted behind the front spar, and a seventh slat at the extended wingtip. They both have enlarged horizontal stabilisers with greater span and chord, and the A330-200 fin, which gives a 1m increase in height and a 10% chord extension. A 1.6m centre-fuselage plug accommodates the additional wing chord. The A340-500 has a 1m plug in the rear cabin, and 0.53m ahead of the fuselage centre-section, while the A340-600 has a 3.2m plug in the rear cabin and a 5.87m plug ahead of the wing leading edge. The provision for foreplanes had been deleted and the centre main landing gear had become a single four-wheeled bogie, rather than installing two separate legs to accommodate the 356-tonne MTOW of the baseline A340-500/600.

The requirement was for lower unit costs and longer range with a need to match the airline needs of take-off distance, range, capacity and flightdeck configuration. One of the major challenges was in effect to design a high-performance racing car to carry fuel for up to 17hr for the last hour of flight. An extra 500 miles of range adds to the costs because of the increased take-off weight and thrust required. The strongest support for the A340-500 came from the Asia-Pacific airlines who had requirements to fly from Hong Kong to New York, and between South East Asia and the US West Coast. The A340-600 was of greater interest to European carriers as a replacement for the Boeing 747-200/300s. The timetable for the new A340 programme called for the start of production in the third quarter of 1998, with final assembly of the first aircraft starting in early 2000. Flight testing would begin in the third quarter of 2000, with certification and the first delivery about 12 months later.

By May 1997, the power being offered by the P&W PW4557 and R-R Trent 500 engines was already achieving a bonus of higher operating weights and additional fuel capacity to give 935km (500nm) more range. The baseline -500 was configured to carry 313 passengers in a three-class layout over ranges of 15,360km, and required engines developing 236kN (53,000lb), while the longer -600 with 378 seats, but

Above: Singapore Airlines became the launch customer for the A340-500 with orders for five aircraft and options on a further five. *Airbus Industrie*

Above: Virgin Atlantic was also the joint launch customer for the high-capacity long-range A340-600, when a letter of intent was signed for eight aircraft in October 1997. *Rolls-Royce*

1,850km less range, required engines of 249kN. Later versions would be powered by 276kN engines, and the new enlarged wing gave adequate increased fuel capacity.

With the selection of the Rolls-Royce Trent 500 engine in June 1997, developing 250kN (56,000lb) thrust for both new versions of the A340, the programme could be formally launched in the market place. Airbus announced the commercial launch of the new programme at the Paris Air Show in June, to allow the aircraft to be offered to the airlines in order to determine the formal interest, although Virgin Atlantic and Air Canada had committed informally. A full industrial launch was planned for September or October 1997, but was conditional on a significant number of launch commitments. When compared with the 747-400, the long-range A340-600 would have 60% more cargo capacity and offer airlines 15% lower trip costs. The Trent 500s would provide 8% improved specific fuel consumption and 25% reduced maintenance costs over the 747-400, with noise levels less than the current A340s. The new Messier-Dowty centre main landing gear would be steerable, and the other wing-mounted main gear units and the nose gear would be modified with revised geometry.

By August the potential customers for the A340-600 were pushing Airbus for a higher MTOW

and further improved payload and range performance on the Asia to US destinations. SIA had probably the most demanding requirement for the 206-seat aircraft to operate the 16,260km (8,800nm) from Singapore to Los Angeles. Cathay was looking for an aircraft capable of flying from Hong Kong to New York and Toronto, ideally combining the 14,000km range with the larger 382-seat capacity of the shorter-range A340-600. Higher-thrust engines would allow the MTOW to be increased to 390 tonnes, but the Trent 500s developed 236kN although certification would take the aircraft up to a 267kN powerplant. In discussion was a higher-growth-weight version of the A340-500, with MTOW increased by 9 tonnes to 365 tonnes.

To satisfy the demanding requirements of airlines such as SIA, Airbus completed a review of the baseline specification of the planned new A340 versions in September 1997, increasing the design weight and extending the range by about 370km (200nm). One of the changes was to retract the centre undercarriage units forward instead of aft, allowing space for two more pallets in the rear cargo hold. The MTOW on both the A340-500 and -600 was increased by 9 tonnes to 365 tonnes, while maximum landing and zero fuel weights were up by 6 tonnes to 236 tonnes and 220 tonnes respectively on the -500, and 254

Above: Egyptair already has A340-300s in service and has placed orders for two A340-600s, with options on two more. *Airbus Industrie*

tonnes and 240 tonnes on the -600. This allowed the ultra-long-range -500 to carry 313 passengers up to 15,800km (8,500nm), with a similar gain for the -600 to 13,875km. No further power was required from the Trent 553, which would develop 236kN (53,000lb) of thrust, but MTOW could be increased to 390 tonnes on a developed version of the engine with 267kN thrust. The Singapore Airlines requirement was for a 206-seater capable of flying nonstop the 16,260km (8,800nm) from Singapore to Los Angeles, and the competition came from the projected Boeing 777-200X.

Both Airbus and Boeing have been studying for some years a follow-on large-capacity airliner from the existing Boeing 747s, the one area where Airbus do not yet have a comparable aircraft. The Airbus proposals are based around a double-deck ultra-wide-bodied airliner eventually capable of carrying up to 1,000 passengers over busy long-range routes. One of the logistical problems for such a large aircraft would be how to bring the major assemblies together from all over Europe, since they would be too large to transport by road or rail. One alternative would be to use a coastal site for final assembly and bring the parts in by sea, but not all the manufacture is undertaken near a coast which would be accessible to suitable shipping. Therefore, Super Airbus Transport International (SATIC) considered a large-volume aircraft similar in concept to the Beluga, based on the smaller A300-600ST but using the A340 airframe. The studies ranged from

a simple side cargo-door-equipped A340 for normal commercial cargo operations, to the full Beluga Mega Transporter based on the A340-300. Another commercial cargo version allows access to the main deck through an upward-opening door above the nose, and the flightdeck below the main deck floor level. For the carriage of the A3XX sub-assemblies, such as the fuselage sections, the cargo bay diameter would need to be increased from the existing Beluga diameter of 7.4m to at least 10m. Although the proposals were initially based on the A340-300, an even larger version could be developed from the A340-500/600 when they became available from 2002.

By late October, Airbus was making strong efforts to gain sufficient orders to launch the A340-500/600 programme, with commitments by letter of intent from Air Canada for five aircraft, and from Virgin for eight. The six target airlines were Egyptair, Emirates, EVA Air, Lufthansa, Swissair and Singapore Airlines. All six airlines were in the final stages of their evaluations, and three already operated earlier models of the A340. Because neither Airbus nor Boeing could achieve the particularly demanding SIA specification, the airline had reduced the number of passengers from 206 to between 190 and 195.

In early December, the European consortium received board approval for the full industrial launch of the $2.9 billion A340-500/600 programme with a first flight of the A340-600 planned for January 2001. The first A340-500 was due to follow in July 2001. By this time Airbus had some 100 commitments from seven airlines, including Lufthansa, Swissair, Emirates and Egyptair, although some were subject to confirmation. Deliveries were planned for the -600 to Virgin in early 2002, followed soon after by the -500, taking Airbus into the 300 to 400-seat long-range airliner market for the first time.

To help with the investment in the new Airbus programme, British Aerospace received launch aid from the British government in February 1998. This £123 million ($200 million) repayable loan, representing about one third of BAe's share of development costs for the programme, gave the British taxpayer an investment in this profitable programme, and was in addition to a £200 million loan to Rolls-Royce to help with the engine development. Funds were already being paid back from the original loans for the A320 and A340, and although BAe could have financed the development itself, it was helpful to have a long-term British Government commitment to the European partnership.

At the Farnborough Air Show in September 1998, current and future airlines for the A340 programme met to discuss design options for the new generation of aircraft. The cockpit is expected to have active matrix LCD displays, and systems design was programmed to be complete by the year end. Focus groups were working in parallel with design/build teams to ensure a mature service-ready aircraft at service entry.

The basic wing aerodynamic design had been completed by January 1997, and since then wind tunnel tests have been conducted by Aérospatiale, BAe and Daimler-Benz to fine-tune the overall design. The engine nacelle inlet and pylon design were also finalised, and the design was completed by the end of the year.

The larger fin developed for the A330-200 twinjet had been selected for the more powerful Trent-powered A340-500/600 to cope safely with the engine failure case. The new larger tailplane will be made entirely of carbonfibre-reinforced plastic, unlike the current units which are a carbonfibre/aluminium hybrid. The new aircraft will make use of new structural materials in a number of other areas, including the replacement of the existing metal rear pressure bulkhead by a carbonfibre structure. The current steel engine

pylons will be replaced by mainly titanium structures, and to meet the weight targets for the aircraft, new lightweight materials will be used in the wing.

The new wing incorporates a three-frame (1.6m) wing-box extension with a tapered insert along the front spar, and a 1.6m wingtip extension, plus the existing 2m winglets, taking overall span to 63.3m. The wing area has been increased by 20%, and combined with the larger centre-section this will increase fuel capacity by 38%. The A340-500 features an extended centre-section fuel tank, increasing fuel capacity by 50% over the A340-300. The aircraft have been developed within the economies of the family, the new wing retaining commonality for spares with the earlier versions, even though the all-up weight has been increased by 100 tonnes.

The tapered insert increases the wing sweep from 30° to 31.5°, and the greater chord without an increase in depth should result in the cruising speed increasing in all conditions to M0.83, compared to the current M0.82. This will be the largest wing ever produced for a civil aircraft in Europe, and BAe will be investing up to £70 million ($113 million) in a purpose-built production line at the large Chester factory.

With a length of 75.3m, the A340-600 will be the world's longest airliner, and with the Messier-Dowty landing gear remaining at the same height, the long fuselage could bring some problems with tail scrape. This will probably be solved by software changes to the flight control system.

Rolls-Royce planned to start ground runs of the new Trent 500 engines in the second quarter of 1999, with certification expected by the end of 2000. Flight testing will be undertaken with one Trent 500 replacing a CFM56 on the A340-300 development aircraft before the maiden flight of the first A340-600.

Fabrication of the first A340-600 began in July 1998, with metal being cut for the wing centre-section box. Final assembly by Aérospatiale at Toulouse is planned to begin in the second quarter of 2000, integrated with the existing A330/A340 production in the custom-built Clement Ader assembly hall. Two further examples of the wing-to-fuselage mating stations will be built since the current versions will not be able to accommodate the new aircraft, although the new ones will be

Left: For the ultra-long-range flights being planned for the A340-500/600s, underfloor sleeper cabins have been offered by Airbus for the first class passengers, but none has yet been adopted, although Virgin Atlantic did show some interest. *Airbus Industrie*

development programme. By using the FBW, the control laws can be modified to represent the new developments, with telemetry playing an important part in making every flight more productive. One of the inboard pylons will be used to flight test the Rolls-Royce Trent 500 when the first flight development examples become available, significantly shortening the flight testing of the new A340-500/600s.

Although Airbus has long been enthusiastic about twinjet operations over long-range routes, the Erops conditions may be too restrictive for ultra-long-range flights. As an example, a series of alternate Category 1 standard airfields would need to be available for safe diversion, and these are simply not in existence on transpolar or transpacific routes. Erops can cause delays for passengers and add substantially to operating costs, which can be avoided on the Erops-free four-engined A340.

With the latest versions firmly established in development, Airbus plans to test the baseline aircraft first, before looking at even greater performance capabilities further into the future. The wing structure has the capability for higher weights, which when combined with more powerful versions of the Trent, will also increase the payload/range capability, keeping the aircraft competitive well into the future.

capable of accepting the existing A330/A340 variants. The plan is for the production rate of the A340-500/600 to reach four per month in 2004, in addition to the existing A330/A340, the new aircraft being complementary to the existing A340-300 rather than a replacement.

Airbus Industrie worked with the potential launch airlines using full-scale models of the nose, including the cockpit, engines and other maintenance intensive areas to test accessibility in practical terms. A centralised maintenance system, developed on the A320, links all the systems, logging and displaying all faults and the location. Working groups including the customers were established to cover all aspects of the flightdeck, cargo handling and maintenance.

The first A340 is being used in a programme of progressive development of the new long-range versions in advance of these joining the flight

APPENDICES

I. Specification

	-200	-300	-500	-600
Wingspan	60.30m/197ft 10in	60.30m/197ft 10in	63.5m/208ft 4in	63.5m/208 ft 4in
Length	59.39m/194ft 10in	63.65m/208ft 10in	67.8m/222ft 5in	75.3m/247ft 1in
Fuselage diameter	5.64m/18ft 6in	5.64m/18ft 6in	5.64m/18ft 6in	5.64m/18ft 6in
Height	16.74m/54ft 11in	16.74m/54ft 11in	17.8m/58ft 5in	17.8m/58ft 5in
Wing area	363.1sq m/3,908.4sq ft	363.1 sq m/3,908.4sq ft	437sq m/4703.9sq ft	437sq m/4703.9sq ft
Empty weight	123,085kg/271,350lb	126,873kg/279,700lb	170,400kg/375,658lb	177,000kg/390,208lb
Max payload	45,915kg/101,225lb	47,127kg/103,900lb	43,300kg/95,457lb	55,800kg/123,015lb
Max take-off weight	257,000kg/566,575lb	271,000kg/597,450lb LR	365,000kg/804,666lb	365,000kg/804,666lb
Max landing weight	181,000kg/399,025lb	190,000kg/418,875lb LR	236,000kg/520,278lb	254,000 kg/559,960lb
Fuel capacity	140,000lt/30,796imp gal	140,000lt/30,796imp gal	213,120lt/46,880imp gal	195,620lt/43,031imp gal
Powerplants	CFM56-5C2	CFM56-5C4	Trent 553	Trent 556
Thrust	138.8kN/31,200lb	151.2kN/34,000lb	236kN/53,000lb	249kN/56,000lb
Max cruise	M0.86	M0.86	M0.86	M0.86
Operating cruise	M0.82	M0.82	M0.83	M0.83
Range	13,806km/7,450nm	13,149km/7,100nm	15,750km/8504nm	13,900km/7,506nm
Passengers	263	295	313	380
Pax one class	-	440	440	485

II. Airbus A340 Sales (Correct to 1 May 1999)

Operator	Type	Order	Options	Remarks	Operator	Type	Order	Options	Remarks
Air Canada	-300	17		ILFC lease	Iberia	-300	8	4	
Air Canada	-500	2			ILFC	-300	3		
Air Canada	-600	3	10		ILFC	-300E	12		
Air China	-300	3			ILFC	-500/-600	5	5	
Air France	-200	3			Kuwait Airways	-300	4		
Air France	-300	19			Lufthansa	-200	6		
Air Lanka	-300	3			Lufthansa	-300	14		
Air Mauritius	-300	6			Lufthansa	-600	10		
All Nippon Airways	-300	5	5		Northwest	-300	24		Cancelled
Austrian Airlines	-200	2			Olympic	-300	4		
Austrian Airlines	-300	2			Philippine Airlines	-200	4	4	
Brunei government	-300	6			Philippine Airlines	-300	4		
Brunei government	-8000	1		Not delivered	Qatar government	-200	1		
Cathay Pacific	-300	6	6		Sabena	-200	2		
Cathay Pacific	-300E	16			Sabena	-300	3		
China Eastern	-300	5			Singapore Airlines	-300	14	6	
China Southwest	-300	3			Singapore Airlines	-300E	10	20	
Continental Airlines	-300	7		Cancelled	Singapore Airlines	-500	5	5	
Egyptair	-200	3			Swissair	-600	5	4	
Egyptair	-600	2	2		TAP Air Portugal	-300	4		
Egyptian government	-200	1			THY Turkish Airlines	-300	7		
Emirates	-500	6	6		Undisclosed	-200/-300		5	
EVA Air	-500/-600	6	6	Cancelled	UTA	-300	7		Taken over
GECAS	-300	5							by Air France
GPA	-300	4			Virgin Atlantic	-300	10		
Gulf Air	-300	6	6		Virgin Atlantic	-600	10		

III. Airbus A340 Production

MSN	Model	Customer	Reg.	F/f	Del.	Remarks
0001	300	Airbus	F-WWAI	25.10.91		1st prototype
0002	311	Airbus	F-WWAS	3.2.92	30.5.97	To Virgin as G-VHOL, Jetstreamer
0003	311	Airbus	F-WWDA	15.6.92	7.7.97	To Virgin as G-VSEA, Plane Sailing

MSN	Model	Customer	Reg.	F/f	Del.	Remarks
0004	211	Region Air	F-WWBA	1.4.92	28.2.97	Leased to Air Vietnam
0005	311	Air France	F-GLZA	31.7.92	17.8.93	
0006	211	Lufthansa	D-AIBF	20.7.92	16.11.93	Luebeck
0007	311	Air France	F-GLZB	18.1.93	26.2.93	
0008	211	Lufthansa	D-AIBA	7.12.92	29.1.93	Nuernberg
0009	211	Lufthansa	D-AIBB	7.1.93	11.3.93	To Brunei gov 3.93 as V8-JP1/V8-AM1
0010	211	Sabena	F-GNIA	19.3.93	13.5.93	Lsd to Air France, destroyed by fire CDG 20.1.94
0011	211	Lufthansa	D-AIBC	3.2.93	5.4.93	Leverkusen
0013	311	Virgin	G-VBUS	19.10.93	26.11.93	Lady in Red
0014	211	Sabena	F-GNIB	2.4.93	9.6.93	Lsd to Air France, to Sabena as OO-SCW 6.96
0015	311	Virgin	G-VAEL	25.11.93	15.12.93	Maiden Toulouse
0016	311	Virgin	G-VSKY	16.12.93	21.1.94	China Girl
0018	211	Lufthansa	D-AIBD	18.6.93	10.7.93	
0019	211	Lufthansa	D-AIBE	7.7.93	28.8.93	Stuttgart
0020	211	Lufthansa	D-AIGA	16.9.93	13.12.93	Oldenburg
0021	211	Lufthansa	D-AIBH	6.8.93	22.10.93	Recklinghausen
0022	211	Sabena	F-GNIC	26.5.93	25.6.93	Lsd to Air France, to Sabena as OO-SCX
0023	311	THY	TC-JDJ	8.6.93	22.7.93	Istanbul
0024	311	Lufthansa	D-AIGB	27.10.93	30.11.93	
0025	311	THY	TC-JDK	23.6.93	10.8.93	Isparta
0026	211	Qatar	A7-HHK	21.4.93	28.5.93	
0027	311	Lufthansa	D-AIGC	5.10.93	2.12.93	Wilhemshaven
0028	311	Lufthansa	D-AIGD	4.1.94	28.1.94	
0029	311	Air France	F-GLZC	21.7.93	30.9.93	
0031	211	Air France	F-GLZD	23.7.93	11.10.93	Lsd to Air Tahiti 11.98 as F-OITN
0032	311	Air Lanka	4R-ADA	24.5.94	19.9.94	
0033	311	Air Lanka	4R-ADB	20.7.94	6.10.94	
0034	311	Air Lanka	4R-ADC	3.3.95	22.3.95	
0035	311	Lufthansa	D-AIGF	13.4.94	16.5.94	
0036	312	Gulf Air	A40-LA	8.4.94	17.5.94	Dhofar, lsd to PAL & Sabena as OO-SCU
0038	211	Air France	F-GLZE	24.1.94	21.2.94	To AOM Minerve SA
0039	312	Gulf Air	A40-LB	25.5.94	18.7.94	Al-Fatah, lsd to Air Mauritius
0040	312	Gulf Air	A40-LC	1.7.94	1.8.94	Doha, lsd to PAL
0041	312	TAP	CS-TOA	25.11.94	22.12.94	Ferrei Mendes Pinto
0043	211	Air France	F-GLZF	17.2.94	18.3.94	To AOM Minerve SA
0044	312	TAP	CS-TOB	14.12.94	22.12.94	
0046	212	Brunei	V8-BKH	25.2.94	31.3.94	
0047	311	Sabena	F-GNID	9.2.94	8.3.94	Lsd to Air France, to Sabena as OO-SCY
0048	312	Air Mauritius	3B-NAT	26.4.94	18.5.94	Paille-en-Queue, to Air Jamaica 3.99
0049	311	Air France	F-GLZG	18.3.94	8.4.94	
0051	311	Sabena	F-GNIE	23.3.94	27.4.94	Lsd to Air France, to Sabena as OO-SCZ 4.97
0052	311	Lufthansa	D-AIGH	30.6.94	12.8.94	
0053	311	Lufthansa	D-AIGI	17.10.94	31.10.94	
0056	311	Lufthansa	D-AIGK	7.12.94	23.12.94	
0057	311	THY	TC-JDL	21.4.94	28.7.94	Ankara
0058	311	Virgin	G-VFLY	5.10.94	24.10.94	Dragon Lady
0061	212	Egypt gov	SU-GGG	21.4.94	22.2.95	
0063	211	Cathay	VR-HMR	14.9.94	26.10.94	To PAL as F-OHPF 9.96
0074	211	Cathay	VR-HMS	27.10.94	28.11.94	To PAL as F-OHPG 11.96
0075	211	Austrian	OE-LAG	2.2.95	28.2.95	Europe
0076	312	Air Mauritius	3B-NAU	21.10.94	28.10.94	Pink Pigeon
0078	311	Air France	F-GLZH	5.1.95	18.7.95	
0079	312	TAP	CS-TOC	17.2.95	24.4.95	Wenceslau de Moraes
0080	211	Cathay	VR-HMT	5.12.94	6.2.95	To PAL as F-OHPH 1.97
0081	211	Austrian	OE-LAH	27.1.95	27.2.95	Asia
0084	312	Air France	F-GLZI	12.7.95	7.8.95	
0085	211	Cathay	VR-HMU	3.3.95	4.4.95	To PAL as F-OHPI 3.97
0088	313	Air Canada	C-FTNQ	19.1.95	15.6.95	ILFC lease
0089	313	Kuwait	9K-ANA	8.3.95	29.3.95	Warba

MSN	Model	Customer	Reg.	F/f	Del.	Remarks
0090	313	Kuwait	9K-ANB	23.3.95	7.4.95	Al Sabahiya
0091	312	TAP	CS-TOD	28.3.95	24.4.95	D Francisco de Almeida
0093	313	Air Canada	C-FTNP	15.3.95	23.6.95	ILFC lease
0094	312	Air Mauritius	3B-NAV	13.3.95	31.3.95	ILFC lease, Kestrel
0097	312	Gulf Air	A40-LD	17.5.95	30.6.95	Abu Dhabi. lsd to PAL
0101	313	Kuwait	9K-ANC	20.4.95	31.5.95	Al-Mobarakiya
0102	312	Cathay	VR-HLD	9.6.95	30.6.95	
0103	312	Gulf Air	A40-LE	23.6.95	13.10.95	Lsd to Egyptair
0104	313	Kuwait	9K-AND	24.5.95	5.7.95	Al Riggal
0114	313	Virgin	G-VSUN	17.1.96	30.4.96	Rainbow Lady
0115	311	THY	TC-JDM	27.2.96	19.4.96	Izmir
0117	313	SIA	9V-SJF	25.8.95	26.10.96	
0123	313	SIA	9V-SJA	25.3.96	17.4.96	
0125	313	Iberia	EC-GGS	31.1.96	29.2.96	Concha Espina
0126	313	SIA	9V-SJB	29.3.96	24.4.96	
0128	313	SIA	9V-SJC	30.5.96	21.6.96	
0129	313	China East	B-2380	18.3.96	15.5.96	
0131	313	China East	B-2381	10.5.96	29.5.96	
0133	312	Gulf Air	A40-LF	7.11.96	4.12.96	Leased to Egyptair
0134	313	Iberia	EC-GHX	16.4.96	10.5.96	
0135	313	Lufthansa	D-AIGL	3.4.96	10.5.96	
0136	313	Cathay	VR-HXA	15.5.96	27.6.96	To B-HXA
0137	313	Cathay	VR-HXB	3.6.96	20.6.96	To B-HXB
0139	313	SIA	9V-SJD	10.6.96	27.6.96	
0141	313	China East	B-2382	5.7.96	25.7.96	
0142	313	Cathay	VR-HXC	20.6.96	27.8.96	To B-HXC
0145	313	Iberia	EC-GJT	31.7.96	6.9.96	Rosa Chacel
0146	313	Iberia	EC-GLE	10.9.96	18.10.96	Conception Arenal
0147	313	Cathay	VR-HXD	12.7.96	19.9.96	To B-HXD
0149	313	SIA	9V-SJE	4.9.96	17.10.96	
0150	313	Air Canada	C-FYKX	24.10.96	19.11.96	
0151	213	Brunei gov	V8-JBB	23.9.96	11.10.96	
0152	313	Air Mauritius	3B-NAY	28.10.96	13.11.96	
0154	313	Air Canada	C-FYKZ	29.11.96	19.12.96	
0156	212	Egyptair	SU-GBM	8.11.96	26.11.96	Osiris Express
0157	313	Cathay	VR-HXE	18.11.96	19.12.96	To B-HXE
0158	313	Lufthansa	D-AIGM	6.1.97	28.1.97	
0159	212	Egyptair	SU-GBN	4.12.96	20.12.96	Cleo Express
0160	313	Cathay	VR-HXF	24.1.97	30.1.97	To B-HXF
0161	313E	China East	B-2383	30.1.97	12.3.97	
0163	313	SIA	9V-SJG	6.12.97	1.3.97	
0164	311	Virgin	G-VAIR	24.3.97	21.4.97	
0166	313	SIA	9V-SJH	6.3.97	27.3.97	
0167	313	Air Canada	C-FYLC	15.3.97	27.3.97	
0168	313	Air France	F-GNIF	2.4.97	17.4.97	
0169	313E	Austrian	OE-LAK	8.4.97	23.4.97	Africa
0170	313	Air Canada	C-FYLD	4.4.97	29.4.97	
0173	313	PAL	F-OHPJ	12.5.97	30.5.97	
0174	313	Air France	F-GNIG	6.5.97	28.5.97	
0175	313	Air Canada	C-FYLG	30.4.97	28.5.97	
0176	313	PAL	F-OHPK	5.6.97	24.6.97	
0178	212	Egyptair	SU-GBO	11.6.97	30.6.97	Hather Express
0179	313	Air Canada	C-FYLU	29.4.97	30.5.97	
0180	313	THY	TC-JDN	1.8.97	19.8.97	Adana
0182	313	China East	B-2384	16.6.97	30.6.97	
0185	313	SIA	9V-SJI	9.7.97	31.7.97	
0186	313	Air France	F-GLZJ	22.8.97	16.9.97	
0187	313	PAL	F-OHPL	28.8.97	25.9.97	
0190	313	SIA	9V-SJJ	17.9.97	16.10.97	
0192	313E	Air China	B-2385	19.9.97	7.10.97	
0193	313E	Iberia	EC-GPB	7.10.97	21.10.97	Teresa de Avila

MSN	Model	Customer	Reg.	F/f	Del.	Remarks
0194	313	Air Mauritius	3B-NBD	30.9.97	22.10.97	Parakeet
0196	313	PAL	F-OHPM	18.9.97	22.10.97	
0197	313	Iberia	EC-GQK	22.10.97	10.11.97	Emilia Pardo Bazan
0199	313E	Air China	B-2386	28.10.97	21.11.97	
0201	313E	Air China	B-2387	31.10.97	26.11.97	
0202	313	SIA	9V-SJK	18.11.97	11.12.97	
0204	213	Brunei Gov	V8-AC3	19.12.97	27.11.98	
0207	313	Air France	F-GLZK	5.12.97	2.1.98	
0208	313	Cathay	B-HXG	16.1.98	12.2.98	
0210	313	Air France	F-GLZL	23.1.98	20.2.98	
0212	313E	SIA	9V-SJL	4.2.98	19.3.98	
0213	313	Lufthansa	D-AIGN	20.2.98	12.3.98	Solingen
0214	313E	Virgin	G-VPOW	25.2.98	16.3.98	African Queen
0215	313E	SIA	9V-SJM	13.3.98	23.4.98	
0216	313	Air Canada	C-GBQM	24.4.98	14.5.98	ILFC lease
0217	313	Iberia	EC-GUP	29.4.98	26.5.98	Augustina De Aragon
0218	313	Cathay	B-HXH	12.3.98	31.3.98	
0220	313	Cathay	B-HXI	2.6.98	23.6.98	
0221	313	Iberia	EC-GUQ	3.6.98	25.6.98	Beatriz Galindo
0225	313E	Virgin	G-VFAR	18.5.98	12.6.98	Diana
0227	313	Cathay	B-HXJ	9.6.98	28.7.98	
0228	313	Cathay	B-HXK	2.7.98	6.8.98	
0233	313	Lufthansa	D-AIGO	17.7.98	7.8.98	Offenbach
0235	313	Olympic	SX-DFA	24.9.98	29.1.99	Olympic
0236	313	SIA	9V-SJN	21.9.98	30.9.98	
0237	313	Air France	F-GLZM	24.9.98	23.10.98	
0239	313	Olympic	SX-DFB	31.8.98	29.1.99	Delphi
0242	313	China SW	B-2388	16.11.98	10.12.98	
0243	313E	China SW	B-2389	23.10.98	9.11.98	
0245	313E	Air France	F-GLZN	4.11.98	30.11.98	
0246	313E	Air France	F-GLZO	9.11.98	4.12.98	
0252	313	Lufthansa	D-AIGP	9.12.98	30.12.98	
0257	313	Air Canada	C-GDVV	28.1.99	11.2.99	ILFC lease
0260	313	Air France	F-GLZP	4.2.99	25.2.99	
0263	313	Austrian	OE-LAL	5.3.99	24.3.99	America
0264	313	China SW	B-2390	11.2.99	31.3.99	
0268	313	Air Mauritius	3B-NBE			Paille en Queue
0270	313	THY	TC-JIH	31.3.99		
0273	313E	Air Canada	C-GDVW		1.6.99	
0274	313E	Lufthansa	D-AIGR	28.4.99		
0278	313	Air Canada	C-GDVZ		28.6.99	
0280	313	Olympic	SX-			
0282	313	SIA	9V-			
0289						
0292	313	Olympic	SX-			
0297	313	Lufthansa	D-AIGS			
0302	313	Iberia	EC-			
0304	313	Lufthansa	D-AIGT			
0307	313	Air France				
0310	313	Air France				
0331	313	SIA	9V-			
0360	642	Airbus				A340-600 1st prototype
0363	313	SIA	9V-			
0371	642	Airbus				A340-600 2nd prototype
0376	642	Airbus				A340-600 3rd prototype
0383	642	Virgin				
0391	642	Air Canada				

This tabulation is based on information available at the time of writing. Because the A330 and A340 are built on basically the same production lines, the allocation of a manufacturer's serial number can be left fairly late to match demand.